Dedicated to the memories of my mother and my sister Patsy

They Always Test Us On Things We Haven't Read

Teen Laments and Lessons Learned

Kathleen Waldron Gershman

Hamilton Books
an imprint of
UNIVERSITY PRESS OF AMERICA,® INC.
Dallas • Lanham • Boulder • New York • Oxford

Copyright © 2004 by
University Press of America,® Inc.
4501 Forbes Boulevard
Suite 200
Lanham, Maryland 20706
UPA Acquisitions Department (301) 459-3366

PO Box 317
Oxford
OX2 9RU, UK

Library of Congress Control Number: 2004108373
ISBN 0-7618-2931-8 (paperback : alk. ppr.)

∞™ The paper used in this publication meets the minimum
requirements of American National Standard for Information
Sciences—Permanence of Paper for Printed Library Materials,
ANSI Z39.48—1992

They place a premium upon preserving the outward appearance of attention, decorum, and obedience. And everyone who is acquainted with schools . . . well knows that thoughts, imaginations, desires and sly activities ran their unchecked course behind this façade.

John Dewy[1]

_____

Dewey, John (1938), *Experience and Education*, NY: MacMillan, p. 62.

Contents

Acknowledgements

I would like to thank my good friend, Bob King, for his thoughtful editing of this book. Margaret Zidon and Jim McKenzie were also kind enough to make constructive criticisms of it early in the writing process.

I appreciate everyone who took the time to read drafts and offer suggestions and assistance: Janet Ahler, Sharon Carson, Carol Christensen, Jolley Christman, Phylline Deraney, Malcolm Evans, Beth Franklin, Steve Goldberg, Sara Hanhan, Steve Harlow, Joanne Harris, David Hird, Brent Hurtig, Sharon Johnson, Vicki Johnson, Marilyn Klug, Amanda Madar, Eric Marin, Cindy Mahoney, Jo Murphy, Viann Pederson, Vito Perrone, T.C. Perry, Harriet Powers, Jeffrey Shultz, Deb Scott, Philip Smith, Denise Twohey, Paula Cooke Williams and Stuart Uggen.

Mary Harris, Dan Rice and Dick Landry of the University of North Dakota were generous in helping me find time for this research. My inestimable mentor, the late Professor Donald W. Oliver, provided wonderful support. And special thanks to Rilla Anderson for her hard work and commitment.

Thank you to the teachers and administrators in the three high schools who let me into their classrooms with unfailing courtesy and good cheer. To the four students who found the time to talk to me week after week: you made many memorable contributions to this work and I appreciate it.

To my loving siblings Richard, Joie and Peggy, thank you for your sincere nagging, I mean interest.

And to my twin pillars of strength and faith, Hal and Leonora, my heartfelt gratitude.

statistically the results are not encouraging: students describe themselves as having feelings ranging from bored (57%) to worried (48%) to angry (37%).[5]

The two cities (pop. 50,000 and 60,000) where I did the research for this book are located in the safest of the fifty states,[6] North Dakota, with newspapers that publish long honor rolls quarterly, communities that crowd into gymnasiums and auditoriums, teachers who are hardworking, and taxpayers who proudly pay them some of the highest salaries in the state. Not surprisingly, these three schools have graduation rates (around 98%) that are the source of great civic pride. Well over half of their graduates go on to some sort of post-secondary education, and with enrollments ranging from 800–950 students, they average 5 National Merit finalists a year. But even ostensibly successful schools can have students who are quite disaffected. While 39% say they love school or like it a lot; and 39% like it "just somewhat,"about a quarter of them, 22%, report that they either hate school or like it just a little.[7] The latter population is the general focus of the description and discussion in the following chapters.

I thought eleventh graders would be a good source for learning more about this uncomplicated-*looking* academic environment. I thought tenth graders might be nervous about arriving and twelfth graders might be anxious to get going. Eleventh graders would be poised in the middle of their high school career, experienced but not jaded. So for the better part of a year I observed classes in required and elective subjects. I talked to girls and boys, aiming for a good cross-section of students with poor, average and high grades. I talked with those with jobs and extra-curricular interests in things like sports or the arts, and to those with no apparent school interests at all. Every interview lasted at least an hour; names of the students, teachers and schools have been changed. I hoped my continuing presence over time would accomplish trust with students who talked with me. And seeing students in their daily environs informed my questions and provided me with hundreds of pages of field notes. From these I have selected vignettes on the following pages to illustrate the perceptions that the students described. And although I have my own memories of attending and teaching high school, I did my best not to rely on them to inform my interpretation. In fact, to me their classroom experiences often seemed humorous or unfair or in ways that the students did not perceive them to be, so for example where I might see a busy teacher as someone treading water as fast as she can, students assess her as crabby or dismissive.

I was moved unexpectedly by much of what students said. Now as I read through the transcripts to write this, I find myself hoping all is well with these trusting teens, so far from the woolly cocoon of their school. I am thankful to all of the high school juniors who were good enough to speak to a stranger with honesty and humor. My hope is that after hearing what they say ("*Par-*

ents don't understand the pressure, other than just grades, that's going on in school!") adults might rethink their expectations of secondary education. Maybe some modest reconstructions, salutary for school lives, could follow.

The students I interviewed did not hold all of the feelings described here all of the time, but they would recognize them as typical of their age group. Recognizing these feelings, even if not claiming them as precisely descriptive of their own, is what makes theirs a cohesive sub-culture. For example, "teacher favoritism" came up often in interviews as a response to prompt cards such as, "frustrated," "angry" or "strong conviction." This idea of "pets" relates to what students perceive as a lack of democracy in schools. A large majority of "Grungies" believe teachers have pets; and virtually no "Prep" ever mentions them. But we can infer that students are aware of pets as an issue, just as they are aware of cliques as an issue, though people never describe themselves as members of one. The group as a whole understands its own ethos[8] in these matters (and more of an ethos is felt than can be observed). But at the same time, sharing that ethos does not mean a strict predictability of a member's feelings at a given moment. It only means one can recognize, by contrast, a new and naïve member.

Some might say that a report about how students describe well-regarded schools in small Midwestern cities will have little relevance to them. But the contrasts between these schools and others should illumine a fundamental fact common to both, that getting adolescents to fall in love with learning is a daunting challenge. It doesn't much matter where the people live who are trying to do it. Walker Percy observed that the "The only way to write about America in general is to write about America in particular."[9] The particulars described here will be recognizable to adolescents in other places, if not always to their teachers or their teachers' educators. I believe that when a seventeen year-old in the Great Plains says with a sigh, "Friends are a great stress reliever," a seventeen year-old in the inner city gets it immediately; that when a rural student confides, "I don't get the concept of anything," an urban counterpart understands.

In the concluding chapters I make no attempt to relate students' perceptions to the larger theoretical frameworks of anthropology or sociology.[10] I am more interested in researching the relative presence of teacher, student and subject in the immediate pedagogical moment. If we listen carefully we hear those vital entities converging and going their separate ways, over and over again in a given class period. This is where I think school reform has to begin, with a philosophical discussion of these intersects of feeling, or what Whitehead calls "prehensions."[11]

Many of my own prehensions that year of research are vivid in my mind. I remember the stifling August day I observed in the first class, "American

Literature." As I headed for the back row, the amiable teacher indicated my presence, "from the university . . . interview . . . what it's like to be a junior. . . ." Several intoned sagely to neighbors, "Ask *me*." The next day I went in for a second observation and sat in the same seat. A smiley girl looped around: "Well? she whispered, "Do you think we're interesting?" I nodded, grateful to her for the welcome. I almost shook my head and said, *Do I ever,* but then she'd have seen that I was already depressed.

NOTES

1. Brigham, D.L. (1989), "Dewey's Qualitative Thought As Exemplary Art Education," *Art Education, 3*, 14–22.

2. "Neither in conceptual work, nor in empirical research nor in the conventional wisdom and discourse of practice does the subjective experience of students as they are engaged in learning figure in any central way," in Erickson, Frederick and Jeffrey Shultz (1992), "Students' Experience of the Curriculum,' in *The Handbook of Research on Curriculum*, Philip Jackson, ed., American Educational Research Association, p.466.

3. For examples of an etic perspective see: Chang, Heewon (1992), *Adolescent Life and Ethos: An Ethnography of a US High School*, London: Falmer Press; Eckert, Penelope (1989), *Jocks and Burnouts: Social Categories and Identity in the High School*, NY: Teachers College.

4. For the emic perspective of schooling see: Cusick, Philip (1973), *Inside High School: The Student's World*, NY: Holt, Rinehart and Winston; Gilbert, Robert N., and Mike Robins (1998), *Welcome to Our World: Realities of High School Students*, Thousand Oaks: Crown; Grant, Gerald (1988), *The World We Created At Hamilton High*, Cambridge: Harvard University Press; Salzman, Marian and Teresa Reisgies (1991), *Greetings from High School: Teenspeak About High School and Life*, Princeton: Peterson's Guides.

5. The Shell Poll (1999), "Teens Under Pressure, Coping Well," Vol. 1, 4, summer. Full results of this poll of 1,015 randomly selected high school students including 261 Freshmen, 260 sophomores, 262 juniors and 232 seniors are found at <http//www.countonshell.com/shell_poll.html.

6. Source: Uniform Crime Reports, Federal Bureau of Investigation, Washington, DC, 1998.

7. The Shell Poll (1999).

8. Researchers conclude that each school has its own ethos which is largely responsible for its success or failure . . . schools with a good ethos had several things is common: teachers got along well with students and their expectations of students were high. They assigned homework regularly, marked it rapidly and returned it with helpful comments. They came to classes well-prepared, managed classroom time well, moved smoothly from one activity to the next and maintained appropriate dis-

cipline. See Rutter, Michael, et al, (1979/1994): *Fifteen Thousand Hours: Secondary Schools and Their Effects on Children*, Boston: Routledge and Kegan Paul.

9. Lawson, Lewis A. and Victor A. Kramer, eds. (1985), *Conversations with Walker Percy*, Jackson: University of Mississippi Press, p.29.

10. Examples of educational research that connects qualitative data with sociological frameworks are Cusick, Philip (1983), *The Egalitarian Ideal and the American High School*, NY: Longman; Everhart, Robert B. (1983), *Reading, Writing and Resistance: Adolescence and Labor in a Junior High School*, Boston: Routledge and Kegan Paul; Fine, Michele (1991) *Framing Dropouts: Notes on the Politics of an Urban Public School High School*, Albany: State University of New York Press; McLaren, Peter (1994), *Life in Schools: An Introduction to Critical Pedagogy in the Foundations of Education*, 2nd ed., NY: Longman.

11. Whitehead, Alfred North (1929/1978), *Process and Reality*, corrected edition, David Ray Griffen and Donald W. Sherbourne, eds., NY: Free Press; (1933/1964), *Adventures of Ideas*, NY: Free Press; (1938), *Modes of Thought*, NY: Free Press.

Chapter One

Feeling Their Way

Interviewer: Do you like classes where you can have an opinion? Or only those with one, right answer.
Student: No, I think better with an opinion.

***

"In [Plato's] view, the entertainment of ideas is intrinsically associated with an inward ferment, an activity of subjective feeling."

Alfred North Whitehead[1]

What are the main feelings that characterize the experience of going to high school? Students' perceptions deserve our attention because they have powerful implications for behavior. The notion that teachers are "out to get" students (*"They always test us on things we haven't read."*) may be unfounded, but the belief that they are surely will affect the way students react to their teaching; the notion that athletes "all think they're better" may be unfounded, but believing they do will affect the way alienated students deal with them.[2]

School has always had those who disregard the rights of others, but today the schoolyard bully has a different profile. Educators are encouraged to be aware of teens who have characteristics[3] that range from being cruel to animals to being victimized at home. But are teachers in a position to know the backgrounds of all of their students? I think not. Given how many students he averages in a given day the secondary teacher would be hard pressed to evaluate them against predictive criteria. In fact I would suggest that in the present configuration of public schooling there is something of a disconnect, even in a school as bland as a beet field, between what adults intend to happen and how the students there actually experience it all. Miraculous moments of learning and sincere support happen throughout the day, but overall there is a lot of time and money going into an effort that tends to fall flat—unless the intents of public education are to teach punctuality, politeness, orderliness, and respect for extrinsic reward systems[4]—then in that case it is rather successful. And the public would be generally pleased to hear it: a national poll[5] of adults showed that 52% would give schools a good grade of A or B and only 4% would give them a failing grade. But their children are rather too ambivalent about school to be taking full advantage of its academic opportunities. They were not learning much for the sheer love of learning it. Instead these students did a pretty fair job of compartmentalizing the school experience. They loathed school's tedium but loved its communitarianism. They tended to feel indifferent about the curriculum, negative about most of the teaching and positive about the group of which they are a part—when they feel a part of it. (The implications of experiencing no sense of community in school are grim. Even in a quiet place you might feel coerced, bothered, bewildered *and* excluded.) These adolescents didn't necessarily want to know more about academic subjects, but they did want to be there. The challenge would be to take what we know about the latter and have it inform the former: take what makes them want to be a part of school and use it to make them more curious and imaginative; take their interest in communicating with each other and make it a dynamic part of the learning environment.

In teacher education, we have seen an increase in published teacher narratives. The "teacher voice" literature[6] elevates because the teacher comes to see she is not alone, but it also bewilders because it is like hearing half of a story. Where is the student's voice? In the non-academic arena, much of what is written about schools focuses on institutions characterized by morbid statistics. Describing the decline in quality education in economically deprived areas can serve many political agendas.[7] The "troubled school" literature also provides genuinely overworked educators with a culprit for student disaffection from school. How can they do their job well in this social turmoil? If gang membership dramatically empowers the insecure, the debate team has less success recruiting them. When the metal detector and the Missouri Compromise vie for students' attention, the metal detector wins.

These dichotomies do not characterize all schools, of course. Those of us who worry about what works in teaching wonder where it is that the troubled learning environment issues leave off, and the generic "teaching methods" problems start up. Could a look at schools where guns[8] or racial tensions[9] are low-incidence problems be instructive? Could we learn from those quiet schools whose stolid look has remained unchanged for eighty years? What goes on in a school in a middle-class, mid-size community[10] with low crime and high retention, where awards for teacher and school excellence are almost commonplace, teams of math and geography whizzes win national meets, choruses travel across the country to sing in Carnegie Hall or the National Cathedral, cheerleading squads win "spirit" awards and hockey, basketball, volleyball, wrestling, tennis, or speech and debate teams "take state" one year or another? In short, what does school feel like where there are not drastic, pernicious distractions?

Why, you may well ask, if it seems to be working, do we care? The answer does not comfort, even though you learned it from your mother: appearances can deceive. Test scores can be high and the same test-takers can swear off the subject they "excelled" in for the rest of their lives; championship teams can have players who need AA; schools can appear to be successful that have suicidal teens; "placid" and "desperate" can have the same countenance. Like anthropologists in a foreign culture trying to understand the difference between a tic and a wink, we will only come to know if we ask. Schools such as the three I researched—schools that make the parents proud—offer us a rare chance to quietly observe how adolescents seem to feel about being in school. For a teacher educator, this is like a long drink of cold water. The sterile tools of my trade (textbooks on curriculum theory[11]) would be everyone's last choice of reading if stranded on an island. Learning from them taxes the imagination. Curriculum texts obfuscate the presence of the student in the classroom. Like diagrams of dance footsteps, there is not even the remotest hint of rhythm on the paper. No, to understand the feeling of a learning environment, we need to consult real adolescents in real schools.

The adolescents interviewed here were not interested in talking about improving instruction but that didn't mean they had nothing to say about school. In fact they had plenty to say about school, a lot of it in the form of complaints. They had strong opinions about "self-appointed popular people," "weirdoes who spend six hours a night on German" while qualifying as "social idiots," or pop quizzes given by "sneaky teachers." Disregarding how they feel about the learning environment would be as destructive to growth in education as in a relationship. And as it happens, education is about relationships, defined broadly. To Tim, shrugging off a question about academic goals, they are everything: "The reason you *go* to school is to work on your relationships." Tim refers here to friends, girlfriends, teammates, chorus, cast and staff members, teachers, principals, directors and coaches. Yet we will see that even when they talk about the curriculum, students speak in terms of how they relate to the subject, either emotionally (*"I don't care for anything number-related—except for phone numbers"*) or physically (*"when you're, like, totally slapped with all those triangles"*).

They described the ways in which they feel forced to conform to someone else's pedagogical agenda in school, the difficulties they have in accepting the teacher's ideas in English or history, both classes in which they believe they should be allowed to develop ideas of their own. Another form of what they perceived as coercion was the pressure to be well regarded by the teacher in order to get a good grade. Paradoxically the students who accomplish this were often seen as teacher's pets, a despised designation. Another category—not despised but pitied—are what I call the non-pets, students who, by virtue of their low status (typically, poor performance), were the object of a teacher's "freak out." Surprisingly, students objected to few school rules except where they perceive that the infractions are outside the school's purview, such as being caught driving under the influence by police.

"Bothered" (Chapter 3) is an umbrella term I use to describe three general states of mind: bored, angry and stressed. Students reported being bored because of the lack of humor in teachers' anecdotes, lack of novelty in their assignments, and lack of curricular relevance to their lives. Much of their most vivid language described the "agony" of hearing the teacher's voice for fifty-five uninterrupted minutes. This is actually nothing new, of course. But if I expected students to be bored by adults, I was not prepared completely for the object of their anger. Students are angry with each other for being in cliques, that is, for being intolerant of an out-group and for judging others by their appearance. Students also reported stress related to the need to maintain high grades in a competitive atmosphere of relentless testing, and the consequent widespread cheating. I learned that what makes sense across many friendships is the opportunity to party together, often in a place where drinking is expected. The amount of student talk among themselves about drinking—even during the school day—was also unanticipated. Yet the drinking itself is a source of stress: fear of discovery by parent or coach is constant, seeing friends intoxicated, or believing that the most popular kids are the biggest rule breakers is disturbing. Finally students complained about what it feels like to be taught by adults who they believe would not miss the students' presence if the room were empty. Female students speak of male teachers whose neglect of them takes the form of low expectations for their gender. Students were confused by teachers who treat them as if they were in college, using vocabulary that mystifies, or discussing ideas that are too academic to be meaningful to them.

Students suggested that the most important aspect of their lives is the presence of understanding friends; it is what makes school tolerable, if not appealing.[12] They also valued teachers who made them feel recognized.[13] Many of these teachers are described as tough, people who "kick you in the butt." But teacher interest in their progress, even sternly expressed, is a powerful aspect of feeling connected to school. Once again it seems that school works best in those places where students and teacher establish a sense of community[14] together. Unfortunately even in successful schools this happens most often after school, in sports, clubs, or the arts. I believe that schools fail (that is, do not reach their potential as life-shaping institutions) not only because many adults have forgotten the importance of community in schooling but also because students themselves coalesce into a mass that depends for its existence on a teacher out-group. Any observer in a high school will see instances of teacher commitment or kindness, but it is decidedly uncool for a typical student to break out of her[15] culture's resistant mode within the classroom setting and reciprocate. Although students reported feeling coerced, bothered and bewildered - and I could find illustrative examples in my field notes with little effort - it seemed to me that students are also proactive members of a school culture which they themselves help to dichotomize along role lines (*"The teacher doesn't have a lot of grasp on the class because the class's got [sic] a lot more power banded together than he does"*). I have always regretted what I see as the tendency of secondary educators to forget what they learned about child development after they join a school's institutional life; school problems would be ameliorated when teachers remember they are teaching students, not subjects. But any school remediation must consider as well the active role of students in that life. Students' self-impelled disconnection from the teaching aggravates the problem of the subject-centeredness of teachers. The question is, are there ways we could restructure schools so that more authentic dialogue, contributing to a patient understanding of subjects and each other could occur?

NOTES

1. Whitehead, Alfred North (1933/1964), *Adventures of Ideas*, NY: Free Press, p.148.

2. The Thomas Theorem says if people define situations as real, they are real in their consequences; also known as a self-fulfilling prophecy. See Thomas, W.I. and Dorothy Swaine Thomas (1928), *The Child in America: Behavior Problems and Programs*, NY: Alfred Knopf.

3. Characteristics of youth who have caused school-associated violent deaths are: has a history of tantrums and uncontrollable angry outbursts, characteristically resorts to name calling, cursing or abusive language, habitually makes violent threats when angry, has previously brought a weapon to school, has a background of serious disciplinary problems at school and in the community, has a background of drug, alcohol or other substance abuse or dependency, is on the fringe of his/her peer group with few or no close friends, is preoccupied with weapons, explosives or other incendiary devices, has previously been truant, suspended or expelled from school, displays cruelty to animals, has little or no supervision and support from parents or a caring adult, has witnessed or been a victim of abuse or neglect in the home, has been bullied and/or bullies or intimidates peers or younger children, tends to blame others for difficul-

ties and problems s/he causes her/himself, consistently prefers TV shows, movies or music expressing violent themes and acts, reflects anger, frustration and the dark side of life in school essays or writing projects, is involved with a gang or an antisocial group on the fringe of peer acceptance, is often depressed and/or has significant mood swings, has threatened or attempted suicide. See: National School Safety Center (1998) Westlake Village, CA.

4. By developing traits such as conformity and punctuality in their schoolchildren, modern capitalist society manages to get itself "reproduced." See: Bowles, Samuel, and Herbert Gintis, *Schooling in Capitalist America*, NY: Basic Books; Peshkin, Alan (1978), *Growing Up American: Schooling and the Survival of Community*, Chicago: University of Chicago Press.

5. Rose, Lowell (1991), "A Vote of Confidence for the Schools," *Phi Delta Kappa*, v73, no. 2.

6. Freedman, Samuel G. (1991), *Small Victories: The Real World of a Teacher, Her Students and Their High School*, NY: HarperPerennial; Kobrin, David (1992), *In There With the Kids: Teaching in Today's Classrooms*, Boston: Houghton Mifflin; Palonsky, Stuart B. (1986), *900 Shows a Year: A Look at Teaching From a Teacher's Side of the Desk*, New York: Random House; Schulz, Renate (1994), *The Past As Prologue: A Qualitative Study of the Roles of Biography and Teachers' Beliefs in the Practice of Teaching*, NY: Teachers College Press; Sizer, Theodore (1984), *Horace's Compromise: The Dilemma of the American High School*, Boston: Houghton Mifflin.

7. French, Thomas (1993), *South of Heaven: Welcome to High School at the End of the Twentieth Century*, NY: Doubleday; Kozol, Jonathan 1991), *Savage Inequalities: Children in America's Schools*, NY: Crown.

8. For the offense of bringing a firearm to school North Dakota's students are expelled at the lowest rate in the country, 0.8 per 100,000 students per year. Or: with 121,000 students attending 231 public school districts, as well as 110 non-public schools, only one student in the state was expelled for possession of a firearm during the entire 1997–1998 school year). Source: United States Department of Education and Planning and Evaluation Service (1999): *Report on State Implementation of the Gun-Free Schools Act*, Rockville, MD.

9. The minority population in all three schools researched here is less than 2 percent.

10. People who are over 25 in the state of North Dakota number 304,123; 85% (84% nationally) of them are high school graduates; 25% (26% nationally) are college graduates; 66.6% (66.2% nationally) are home owners, and 12.5% (13.3% nationally) are living below the poverty line. The population density is 9 persons (80 persons nationally) per square mile. The median income is $31,764 (U.S. Census, 2000). North Dakota school districts spend an average of $5,830 ($6,800 nationally) per learner per year. Less than half of the schools in the two districts represented in this book have enrollments that qualify for reduced or free meals.

11. For a comprehensive list of this genre see Schubert, William Henry (1984), *Curriculum Books: The First Eighty Years*, NY: University Press of America. 350 pp.

12. 68% of high school students say the best thing about going to school is seeing their friends: The Shell Poll (1999).

13. 49% of students report they have had a teacher who changed their lives: Shell Poll (1999).

14. See: Grant, Gerald (1988), *The World We Created at Hamilton High*, Cambridge: Harvard University Press; Lightfoot, Sara Lawrence (1983), *The Good High School: Portraits of Character and Culture*, NY: Basic Books; Oliver, Donald W. (1976), *Education and Community: A Radical Critique of Innovative Schooling*, Berkeley: McCutchan.

15. In this text the male and female pronouns are used alternately.

Chapter Two

Coerced

"If they push you to read a book, it's not too different than forcing you to listen to music, or forcing you to look at a painting . . . I'd rather, technically, read a *Newsweek*, or just read fake essays, than I would take some work of art and trash it."

Peter, honor student, Grade Eleven

***

"To this day I cannot read *King Lear*, having had the advantage of studying it accurately in school."

Alfred North Whitehead[1]

"Frustrated" describes the main attitude of these students as they passed the halfway point in high school. They are frustrated with the pace of the period (too slow), the pace of the day (too fast), the low enthusiasm of teachers (*"her charisma is not up to par"*) or the high status of other kids (*"jock douche-bags"* who *"think they're on this pedestal"*). Actually they were far less frustrated with school rules than some might expect, certainly far less than their parents, fiery children of the Sixties who could raise a protest parade in the driveway by 8 A.M.[2] The frustration of these children of the new millennium seems more like a low-grade fever, chronically enervating but not life-threatening. It is a vague dissatisfaction that keeps them wary about unwelcome news or unfairness, dissatisfaction with covert, more than overt coercion. Overt coercion is being made, by virtue of explicit rules that threaten punishment, to act in a certain way. Covert coercion is being "made" to act a certain way in order to receive something such as affirming attention, or in order to avoid its opposite.

In general, administrators were mentioned rarely in our conversations, perhaps because the rules students did object to do not seem to be identified with administrators' personalities. Only in a few cases were incidents of perceived mistreatment described at the hands of The Office, people in charge of the building or paperwork. Teachers, of course, were a different issue — uppermost in students' minds at all times. This is no doubt due to the sheer number of hours (about 180 per class, per year) they spend in the company of 6 or 7 secondary teachers. In virtually every conversation we had, students proved the old adage that a teacher teaches as much of herself as she does of her subject (*"Students can tell when a teacher is going to be, like, controlling you. [Students] can smell that. Instantly"*). Students proved this by appearing to be incapable of discussing a subject *apart* from its teacher. The good news for teachers is that they got plenty of credit from students when they learn something. The bad news is that the relationship they have with the teacher got plenty of blame when they don't (*"Right now I have Ms. L. I do not like her at all and therefore I'm doing terrible"*). Teachers might even get the blame for the increase in cheating in schools (*"[The physical education teacher] forces people to cheat at bowling to get an A, because some people don't want to bring their GPA down"*). And the reviews of the teaching are as variable as the students' personalities. Compare two self-described lovers of reading, interviewed the year they took the *same* class from the *same* teacher:

> John: English! Why do I like English so much? I don't know. Probably due to the fact that I've been really lucky with the teachers. I think the teachers have a lot to do with how you do in a class, personally.
> And I've had great teachers, you know, all my life. And so I've been extremely inspired by English! I love reading! I love writing about things.   .

And:

> Brian: Um, English has always been, like, my bad class . . . I alwaysstruggle in English. I never liked my teachers. I heard so many stories about Mrs. D and when I came in I was already saying, no, I'm not gonna like this year . . . I think she took away everything that made reading fun to me . . . I just don't like reading something and taking a test. I like *reading* something. Read it. And enjoy it!

A big difference in students' varied responses to school subjects is the reaction to the evaluation, also seen as teacher-driven. Since students are encouraged from the earliest school days to interpret what they read (because meaningfulness is the key to literacy), they feel disenfranchised when, as seventeen year olds, they have to read what someone else chooses for them, and grade → motivator

then give back the teacher's interpretation of the selection in order to Get The Grade ("*The grade is a game. You play the game and get the points and get the grade*"). After all those years of being told to think about what they are reading, they are then told what to think of it ("*. . . they say "Moby Dick" is a symbol of [something]. . . [but] that's a bunch of crap. . . I think you should have your own opinion.*") This perception of being disenfranchised is most common among those who place English at the bottom of a list of favorite subjects. High school students—already living with existential questions about who they are supposed to be[3]—have strong feelings about their rights to develop new ideas. The resistance to being idea-compelled is highest in English, the class where students have come to believe a certain latitude for interpretations *should* exist.[4] This resistance is exacerbated by a feeling of betrayal when they see a change from a seeming openness of class discussion to a seeming sameness of response expected on the exam (*"English is English. It's not a right and wrong. It's just reading."*) They think they are roaming free, exploring the range of opinions, only to find themselves corralled.[5] The depth of bitterness over this silent shift—among students who need, or prefer, unambiguous evaluation—is hard to exaggerate. Tom says it vividly:

[The teacher] can read poetry—[written] by some guy who seems like he's on drugs—and what he said could have a million meanings, but *he* says it's got one definite meaning. And if you try to talk to him about it . . . he tries to drive it in your head that, no, that's not right.

There was less of this bitterness in discussions of evaluation in other subjects such as math or science or business. Obviously those classes can be quite challenging for many students, but I believe the constancy of expectations keeps anxiety down. In other words, fear that one did not study hard enough or studied the wrong material has a different quality than the fear that there is a hidden meaning in a question one cannot see. The former is a clear and present danger; the latter is a vague and futile pursuit.

Another perceived coercion, a type of teaching that a student called "trivial pursuit," can be true for history or English—though again, the latter gets the most resentment. Whatever the subject, students can barely endure it, believing themselves to be forced to master, "a lot of things that Just Don't Matter," for purposes of being evaluated. "Trivial pursuit" presents a crisis of trust with the teachers. "*Tests* don't make you learn it," students would say disdainfully, wondering why they understand that and their teachers don't.

Brad: "I've had tests where I have just completely just written crap. I mean I didn't know what I was doing and I just wrote b.s. That's all I did. And she gave me an A. I've had other tests where I really studied for it and I did all I could and she just split hairs, take off all kinds of points for ridiculous things and I'd just get a poor grade when I felt like I'd done a much better job.

Their intuition, reaching across the generations to the authors they read, tells them that the typical mode of teaching is inconsistent with the intent of the person who wrote it.

The loyalty of Peter, an intense honor student and future engineering major who takes home only Advanced Placement (AP) history to read ("*two or three hours a night*"), is clearly with the artist, not his apologists. He had the unusual opinion that school should not be required after the student acquires the basics skills. His indictment is difficult for me as an educator to consider, because he is brilliant student who will one day make a difference in a profession and community:

You know, I just put my finger on what I hate about public schools so bad. It's because it stops that love of learning. That's what it takes away. That's perfect: it stops the love of learning. Well, I mean, no kids read anymore, and no kids *like* poems and stuff. And I know why: because they kill it. If you want one example, we're reading "Our Town" or something, and you're getting to a good point and she says, "Hey! Take that down. You're going to get that in the quiz." [The] "Hey, take that down" stuff doesn't matter! You've [already] had your enjoyment and stuff. And you get to a point where it's being read [out-loud] by a bunch of people who really don't want to read it and it's all *monotone*. "Take that down." "You'll see that in the test." And it becomes work! And I don't think the author ever wanted it to be work.

TEACHERS' PETS

"*Only the brains ask the questions*"

                                                                    Coral, Grade 11

                              ***

"I was beginning to see that Phineas could get away with anything."

                                                                    John Knowles[6]

Students behold their teachers as the people with authority over them all day, every day. This sense of others-in-control reveals a vision of school as a bricked-in place and of themselves as virtually powerless. They were accustomed to this arrangement of course, having been in school by this time for about twelve years. A rearrangement of power is not even on their mental horizons: Cusick[7] found that the formal supra-structure of school was what allowed other informal, but very powerful student social structures to exist. Consequently big changes, with attendant, smaller changes—closer in to where students function—are not really desired by them. Students would no more want to take charge of school than they would their dentist's office; people trained to do that job should be the ones standing next to their chairs. In fact students go to classes with much of the same attitude they have when they get their teeth filled: a necessary, and numbing, experience (though you'd hate to miss the action in the waiting room).

If the social structure does give more power to one group, the other group (even if it doesn't want power) still might have to ingratiate themselves with the higher-ups if they care to access scarce resources. The scarce resource here is the teachers' beatific regard. And beatific regard is blessedly controvertible to the grace of a good grade. The sheer amount of mental energy that students put into ascertaining the teachers' reactions to their personalities was quite substantial. We know adolescents take their relationships seriously, if not always logically (*"At first I thought she would like me 'cuz we're both from St. Louis."*) The amazing thing is how relentlessly students will perceive all aspects of the school world in these terms, even—or I should say especially—in evaluation. Kerry's grade reflects the difference he felt:

> He was not my favorite teacher. . . . He shows a lot of favoritism. He teaches a certain way towards certain kids. The kids who knew what they were doing, he'd always be with them but then the people who didn't [know], he wouldn't really care . . .We were doing [a] genetics [flow chart] and we dropped A, dropped a B and bring down the A and bring down the B and I didn't know what I was doing cuz I had been gone. So he came over here and I go, I don't understand this, and so he had some other kid come over and help me and this kid didn't know what he was doing. So then I said [to the teacher] you need to explain this to me and he just did it *for* me. He didn't say anything to me about it. And then I took a test on it and I failed it. That was him.

A disturbing strain in our conversations was the belief of students that teachers had to like them in order to receive a good grade (*"Most of her grade is based on whether or not she happens to like you."*) (I resisted pointing out that they are probably confusing cause and effect: teachers "like" students who try to do well. Students wouldn't believe it anyway, as they watch others successfully getting on the teachers' good sides, who are cynical about it afterwards to classmates.) The "teacher pet" phenomenon came up so frequently in conversations that I consider frustration about it to be a major theme of the high school experience. Students put the pets into two categories: the first are those who inherit approval by virtue of their appearance, social background, athletic success (*"If these kids that are in hockey and stuff don't get their work done . . . she doesn't get on their case or anything. They can say stuff to her and get away with it;"*) or grade point fame ("*I don't think I've ever seen the guy smile in my life [but] with the smarter kids he just talks to them more*"). These pets are derided as being undeserving of the attention they get "effortlessly."

> Jen: She just has her favorites. It sounds weird but you can just tell, right at the be-
> ginning . . . you could tell right away, right when you go in there the first day of
> that first class, you can just tell . . . it's not so much [that she favors talkers] it's
> more culture for her—going to Minneapolis and seeing the plays and
> dadadadada and New York and everywhere. And . . . some people just don't
> travel very much! But her favorites are just the people that go, like, to Chicago
> to see plays and you know, and I'm just like, "You're not giving everybody a fair
> chance, just because they don't travel like everyone else does," you know?

Not all students who are the pets might enjoy the fame of the designation. They would like to be silently rewarded for their "charm" because their pet status is not appreciated by their peers. In fact, rejection by peers over being a pet was more unbearable than getting a poor grade as a non-pet. I asked every student which would be harder, going to detention or eating lunch with kids they didn't know; I also asked which would be harder, getting dropped from a class or being made to wear a suit and tie or dress and heels every day. Virtually every student said eating with strangers would be harder than detention, and dressing differently from their classmates would be harder than getting dropped from a class. Students want to be special, but on their own terms, not the teacher's. Of course, some students refused to let themselves be coerced into doing any buttering-up at all. They so steadfastly rejected the idea of teachers' pet that they would not even take legitimate steps to get help from a teacher out of fear that they will be perceived by their peers as seeking favor.

An excellent student (below) will agonize over the fact that the journalism teacher appreciated her own good work; it set her apart from her low-scoring pals. This "separation anxiety" ruined Mara's best subject. We see how peer pressure can mitigate against school achievement:

> It's just so irritating. It just makes me so mad [that the teacher likes me]. We
> were supposed to write down journals for our job stations. Well I send mine in
> and it's worth maybe 10 points. And so I got like 13 out of 10 because she
> thought mine was really good. But then some people I'm friends with, they got
> them back and then got D's and F's on them. And I think they're just as good as
> mine were, personally. But I also know that the teacher doesn't like those stu-
> dents . . . and I know she likes me because she's always you know, talking to
> me? And I'm like . . . OK, this puts me in a really bad place. I was so mad at her
> . . . I was looking at their journals and I think they had everything in it that I did.
> I could tell just from reading it and stuff. It's not like [I'm defending them be-

cause] these are my friends. And there wasn't that much difference between theirs and mine that they deserved the F and I deserved over an A. I feel really bad because I know that the teacher doesn't like them and she likes me—I think because they don't do all their homework all the time. You know they're not always perfectly quiet and paying attention. Cuz, I try to pay attention in class! You know, sometimes it gets boring; I [tell them] forget it! But for the most part I make good grades and stuff. I think some of the people were classified as learning deficit (sic) . . . They're not! They just don't do the work. Because just from talking to them [I know that] they *do* hand [homework] in. They're not deficient or slower than other students [but] they don't always go right along with everything. If they have a complaint they really *voice* it. Loudly. And they got so [sic] low grades—When their stuff wasn't any different! That's why I was really mad, cause I'm like, "What position [are] you putting me in?" Cuz I think part of it is, she expects me to get an A and she expects them to get a D or an F.

The second category of pets are those who shamelessly ingratiate themselves with the teacher, actively seeking approval in order to get a grade. Such students were derided as suck-ups. Teachers won't always know when students are patronizing them, or at least students might not see evidence that they do (*"Whoever asks the most questions is a favorite. I know a couple kids that do that just to get on their good side . . . A lot of the time the teacher doesn't really know what's going on"*). Students have spent hours in the company of their teachers and can ascertain their political positions on a variety of topics. The cynical student would not hesitate to use that knowledge to his own grade advantage:

> Robert: That's why we're laughing most of the time because we make up things to put on our papers. Like, I got an A on my speech. We had to write a speech and I did mine on abortion. I did it the cheap way out. . . . I said I was personally against it but I didn't feel that everybody else had to be against it like me, so. And then I used something that I thought would get to [the teacher]: I said that I don't think we should force our puritanistic views on others and that got me an A!

There is a tension between the perspectives on "class participation." While celebrated by the relieved teacher, participation can be regarded quite suspiciously by students themselves. Is someone asking a lot of questions? Then she must be trying to make a good impression to shore up a grade point (rather than fill an informational) deficit. Nobody could possibly, truly *care* about this stuff. Students, at least the "popular" ones, surely would have too much of "importance" on their minds to have genuine questions in class (*"You ask a lot of questions, you're considered kinda a dweeb."*) Goal-oriented students who take studying seriously enjoyed advance-placement classes expressly because they can ask questions there without worrying that peers will regard them as nerds or fakes. But for the average student, real adolescent living is so intense that many regarded interest in bland academia as contrived. And furthermore, schmoozing is easier than studying. At the very least the effect on students of hearing friends admit their own duplicity is that at they become plainly pragmatic about the subtle coercion of grade politics:

> Diane: Yeah, I mean, I have to admit, if you want a good grade, you have to do some portion of brown nosing like coming in to "show" 'em that you at least care and offering to do extra stuff for em, volunteering for stuff and that's only to show 'em that you want the grade and if it comes down to it, and you and this other person have just like two points or something before you get an A or B, I will schmooze the teacher and do the whole extra stuff for her to show her: I want my A; I don't want the B.

The worst thing that the perceived teacher's pet phenomenon does is prevent grass roots development of community. (*"She kind of selected a few people out of the whole class and helped them a lot."*) In one history class I observed, the teacher spent the first ten minutes of every day talking about current events but it quickly turned to sports—the high school or university teams. Two boys in front seats, a golfer and hockey player, were most often involved in this review. One girl, who was quiet there but a standout in Chemstudy, hates history because it was "too easy" and because attention to the teacher's pets fragmented the class:

> Sheila: I mean anyone that could fail *that* class, I mean . . .
> Interviewer: What would you change about it? Is there something he could do as a teacher?
> Sheila: He could make us feel more like a group, you know? He always singles one or two people out. *Always.* That makes a class kind of loose sometimes. Cuz it's always the same one or two people. And it just makes the classroom . . . it's not like a *group.*

TEACHERS' NON-PETS

"If she doesn't like you, she does not like you, and she will grade you that way."

Wanda, Grade 11

***

"You see what's important here, Cochran?" Leon asked, assuming his classroom voice. "School spirit. We have disproven a law of nature—one

rotten apple does not spoil the barrel. Not if we have determination, a noble cause, a spirit of brotherhood."

Robert Cormier[8]

Students were frustrated as well about teachers' disapproval of them. A
thirteen-year school career will include over 40 teachers by the time they
graduate. If he never had a teacher dislike him over the years, a student would
be in an exclusive club—although it would be a membership he would not
flaunt. Students will say indifferently, "Oh, he hated my guts." But they can't
always figure out the root of the "hate," and the mystification around it can
hurt more than the fact of it. They think it renders their efforts at academic
success futile (*"If you don't get along with the teacher, nothing else will
work."*) And then their failure is actually doubled: they fail at the schoolwork,
and they fail at the personal relationship:

> Steve: All through junior high school and high school I've gotten almost straight
> As in every English class. And I've enjoyed English. And this is the first year
> I haven't enjoyed English class. . . I got Cs all [year]. I'll never know why but
> ah, *she didn't like me.* . . In speech class I got a C, the same grade that I did
> in English. And I don't think I deserved a C in that class. I should have at least
> gotten a B but she gave me a C on my final speech. Which I don't think I de-
> served either but that's the grade she gave me so . . .

Teenagers can recognize what one called his "unfavorite" status through
the teachers' language use, the teacher's most powerful weapon (after the
awarding of grades). Non-pets get an unmistakably different tone of voice
than the rest of the class, ranging all the way from slight exasperation to outright hostility. The subtle nuance of "tone" must be the most challenging aspect of language learning. Only after long-term membership in the English
language community can a person hear and apply the tonal difference of:
"Whaaaat?," "Wha*tttt*!," and "what."—signifying the communicative intent
(respectively) of: disbelief, impatience, and the answer to the small child's
question, Know *what*? Language use, that is, vocabulary, syntax, tone, volume, volubility, gesture, facial expression, posture and stance also defines a
social group.[9] And marking their separation from the adult group would be
one good reason why teenagers employ their own "dialect."[10] For example, a
parent's routine reminder to a teenager that homework has to be finished before telephone calls begin, is translated to the phone friend as, "My mom's
freaking. Gotta go."
    Students in this study appropriated an ordinary word and used it repeat-
edly to describe a whole class of teachers' speech. The word is "yell." (*"I
hate it when they yell at you in front of everyone else, to . . . you just feel*

like the biggest moron. I mean, you're not even doing anything wrong!") If
as much yelling occurred as they report, passersby would see the roofs rising off these school buildings every few minutes. Like dogs that wince at
a pitch beyond human perception, students hear a yell when the rest of us
might discern only a stern, or even businesslike, tone. I believe "yell" actually refers less to decibels than to an assertive *impersonality*, a manner
of speech that does not soothe, does not address the "selfhood" of the student. And that hurts when your selfhood is tenuously under construction
("*I don't like to ask questions on math . . . you don't want to go up there
and ask 'em cuz you're afraid they'll flip out on you*"). In one year of observing classes I may have heard a few teachers raise their voices slightly.
But students' perceptions that they are being "yelled at," "totally busted,"
or "drilled on" seemed to be sincerely felt.

Every school and classroom has its unwritten customs, mutually
evolved, often out of the awareness of the members. A newcomer only
comes to know these customs by violating them inadvertently. Learning
rules by breaking them may be the most difficult part of initiation into any
new culture or subculture. In a classroom, it is one quick way to become a
teacher's non-pet. As we have seen, teachers who have non-pets might resort to the freak-out, so-called. Other teachers might not, ever, raise their
voices at their non-pets. How do these teachers get their will accomplished?[11] One way is to be very consistent in the administration of consequences (what elementary students would describe as being a mean
teacher*)* so that eventually all the students are habituated to the teacher's
rules. Where there is not manifest (either sporadic or chronic) opposition
to the teacher's agenda, the class settles into a rhythmic pattern, day in and
day out. While this may sound oppressive—especially if the pattern is entirely dictated to them—secondary students did not actually object to the
routine. Perhaps it is because a consistent disciplinary environment provides fewer dispensations to the dreaded teacher's pets. Even students who
want to assert their own ideas about "Moby Dick" might appreciate a certain strictness. Strict and fair feels better than easy-going but uneven.

Teachers who enforce their rules might be trying also to teach students that
the world will treat them without special consideration. In many visits to the
chemistry class described below, several things were constant across time:
Ken's absentmindedness, the teacher's sarcasm toward him, the no-nonsense
atmosphere of the room, the continual reference to homework, and the
teacher's tendency to disparage a student's individual needs, just as, Mr. T
promises them, the real world surely will. The grouchy-looking Mr. T is firm
with rule breakers, though to the unaffected observer he does not seem to be
yelling. The students involved would disagree:

Chemistry Class, January

Ken comes in to the back of the room all out of breath and says to me, "I always forget my books in my car. I don't know why." Rushes into his seat. There's kind of a hum in here today; kids are all talking at once. Mr. T waits at the head of the classroom; doesn't say a word. Finally someone notices that he's waiting for them.

Teacher: *Don't mind me, the longer you talk the more time we take off the lab.*

At that, everybody turns around and starts listening to him.

Teacher: *In going over your lab sheets, [I found that] your lab was pretty good, your lab work. Your calculations on the other hand were atrocious. (He's walking from the front of the room down the middle aisle. He turns around and stops at Becky, who is still talking to her neighbor): Ah, excuse me?*

Becky: *Nothing.*

Teacher (continues now that he has her attention too): *I want you to grab your lab partner and re-do your calculations. I don't care how sure you are. Re-do them.*

Mr. T circulates around these little groups of two, making sure they're re-doing their calculations. One person in every pair has a calculator in his hand.

Teacher: *You two must be pretty close: you've got three of the same answers— even though they're all wrong.*

Teacher (after they get back in their seats): *Any more people who owe work?*

Steve: *I have one more to pass in.*

Teacher (raises his eyebrows): *This is the last day. You miss school for a school function, you have to get your work in early. And I already gave you an extra day.*

Steve: *But . . .*

Teacher (evenly): *I gave you an extra day.*

Steve (shrugs): *Alright.*

Teacher (goes on): *That's the rule.*

Steve (rejoins the fight): *But I didn't GO to a school function. I didn't go with the team.*

Teacher: *But you went on a school function.*

Class sits motionless, waiting for this mini storm to pass.

Steve (under his breath): *Forget it. (bitterly to the back of his neighbor's head): I didn't know I was going ahead of time. How could I get [the materials to] make up the work?*

His neighbor (turns around to him): *You know you wouldn't have done the assignment anyway, Steve.*

Steve chuckles in rueful agreement.

Mr. T asks students to pass the homework up to be corrected by the student in front of them. Kids in the first seat get up, walk back and give their papers to the kids in the last seat.

Teacher: *Any sign that's missing in the bottom, mark it wrong! You're not doing anybody any favors by being nonchalant about this. Better to get off ½ a point*

*now than 5 points off on Friday. Friday is the exam. Anything wrong, mark the
whole equation wrong. They're going to do it on the test and it's going to hurt
them a lot more. Do them a favor and mark the whole problem wrong.*

Kids work quietly. Ken doesn't have anything on his desk.

Teacher: Where's your homework?

Ken: I forgot it. It's in my locker.

*Teacher: Part of being a junior is remembering your things, remembering not to
leave them in your locker.*

Ken: Can I go get it?

Teacher: No.

Ken: I'm sorry.

*Teacher: Don't apologize to me, apologize to yourself: you're the one who's go-
ing to miss out.*

Ken (contritely): I'm sorry, Ken.

*Mr. T chuckles and whole class laughs. Kids take a long time to go through the
homework, correcting the problems of their neighbors. There's only 15 minutes left for the lab.*

*Teacher: This lab is gonna take 15 minutes, the write-up is gonna take 4½ hours,
no kidding.*

*Everybody groans. Kids go to the lab counters at the back of the room. They
draw a grid with a pencil on the lab surface, some grids are really big, some
are much smaller. With eyedroppers they drop solutions according to the di-
rections, right on the lab table and then they add drops of different solutions
to them and make note of the color changes and the texture changes. Some
kids move through this really fast, almost as though they've done it before, zip,
zip, zip. They work in pairs. Other kids really bring up the rear and they move
very slowly. Two hockey players who are both wearing their uniform shirts because they're playing a team from the neighboring state that night, are lab
partners. When the lab is finished they pull their chairs up next to each other
back in the classroom part of the lab and work out the write-up together.*

Like Mr. T, Mrs. E (below) insists on old-fashioned classroom decorum
and is sincerely interested in students' progress. She reprimands students immediately but apparently does not carry a grudge, a valued attribute in the
adult-in-charge. (Maybe the only thing worse than the teacher's freak-out is
the teacher's smoldering snit.) Although this was not a dynamic class, it was
clear to me that the students appreciated the formidable Mrs. E very much:
her students invariably described her as a great teacher. Students in her class
also seemed quite connected to each other. On a typical day, she would put
notes on two boards all the way around from left to right. Students had to
copy everything down in their notebooks as soon as the class started. Once
done, Mrs. E would talk them, lecture style, through the notes. In the field
note that follows, four hapless students skirt the edge of Mrs. E's non-pet status. All of them know it but one does not escape in time.

English class, February

Desks are all placed carefully at an angle to the door. Teacher's desk is also at an angle on the left side, up front. Room is crowded, desks taken right out to the corners. There are reminders of reading all over the room. "Reading is Nifty" on the bulletin board with dozens of book jackets stapled beneath the sign. Bulletin board shows a big snowman on skis with snowflakes and a mail box that says President's Day on the newspaper inside. Printed sayings hang from the ceiling. These give the room more of a cheery, elementary classroom feel than any other high school classroom I've been in. There are 18 posters around the bulletin boards of types of writers "Critics and Cautionaries" or "Moralists and Musicians" or "Transcendentalists and Romantics" with examples of those types of writers. For example, under Transcendentalists it says, Edgar Allan Poe and William Wordsworth. There are Shakespearean play posters all around the room, and a large poster of Jessica Lange in O Pioneers. *The bulletin board says: Attention, Here's the News. Underneath there are 12 or so scarlet letters done by students, some with embroidery, some painted, some with calligraphy, 4–6 inches tall. Along the back there are 8 computers, 4 facing the room and 4 facing the back wall. On the shelf along two walls there are about 30 or 40 paperbacks, not so many classics but such things as "The Joan Kennedy Story" or "The Landcaster Men" by Janet Daily.*

Several students are wearing shirts or jackets in the school colors. One girl wears a huge colored bow in her hair. They all plan to root for their school in the state hockey tournament that afternoon, wearing their matching colors.

Class is very quiet, writing. Mrs. E whispers and makes faces congenially at the front row kids. I take a seat in the back. (After class Mrs. E says to me "I never even saw you come in!" I say, "Well—I tiptoed.")

Throughout the period the teacher calls up the students one by one to her desk and talks to each one in a low tone about their compositions. She has worked over the drafts with corrections and they will pass in the final draft for district evaluation and storage in a personal portfolio. Every 5 or so minutes the teacher will say a name and someone will get up and go up to the desk. You can barely hear her voice. After awhile the teacher herself gets up and comes over to a boy, puts her hand on his shoulder and talks to him in a low tone. Five or six students stop writing to watch this consultation and advise each other, "She's saying he's got to rewrite. . ." As students return to their desks after their conferences with the teacher, they make a face or whisper their grade to their friends sitting nearby.

One girl in a short pink skirt and white tights and Barbie-big hair calls across two rows to an overweight girl in sweatshirt and sweat pants, "What did you get?" The sweatshirt girl answers "94." The blond girl volunteers, "I got a 100!" Sweatshirt girl says, "Get OUT!" At least ten kids stop writing and listen to this oral report card. When the girls get too loud the teacher looks up and smiles, inclining her head to the side. The girls feel her eyes and stop talking immediately; the whole reprimand is wordless. One boy smiles sardonically twice to his friends in exact imitation of the teacher.

After Mrs. E has conferred with every single student about his paper she says to the entire class,"You should total up your points; I may have made a mistake. We know it's rare for me to do that (sarcastically)." No one chuckles. To Raymond she says, loud enough for everyone to hear, "I changed your grade in the grade book, so you can change it on your paper."

One boy, Mike, is turned sideways in his chair so his long legs stick way out into the aisle of this crowded room; his right elbow is on the desk behind him, left hand writing on his own desk.

Teacher (impeccably groomed and feminine, notices Mike's unorthodox position): Mike?

Mike: I'm just . . .

Teacher (interrupts in a low tone): I'm gonna slam you.

Mike (sputters): But . . .

Teacher (menacingly, eyes narrowing): One more time? Give me a reason.

She stares at him hard. But all the class hoots, delighted at this incongruous standoff. Mike grins a little, then gives up the game, turning his big frame to face front.

Teacher (matter-of-factly in front of everybody): Travis, you're going to get that in today or else you're going to have a 10 point penalty on it.

Travis (nonchalantly): Okay.

Class writes all period and the bell rings. Everybody files out as if obeying a rule to do so in an orderly fashion.

In the final example of Mrs. E's non-pets, Jim frustrates her so much that she sends him off to the office of the assistant principal. But her anger is low key and Jim is unaware of it until his pals clue him in. Absolutely none of what ensues diminishes Jim's loyalty to the stern Mrs. E. The assistant principal, however, receives Jim's unvarnished contempt for his shallow interest in appearances and his militaristic commitment to the hierarchy of principal-teacher-student.

Jim: All teachers bend the rules sometimes. There's always that, there's like two lines. There's like the line where there's all the school rules. And there's the teacher's line. And it can be before or after, you know? So you can cross . . . if you cross the line, you *know[it]*.

Interviewer: How do you learn where the line is?

Jim: You just have to shut up and listen to your teacher. Watch your other students get in trouble . . . In Mrs. E's class I learned that. I always call out answers, and she has to have you raise your hand. But then if you have a smart, intelligent answer and it's right, and you didn't raise your hand, that's OK. But if you did have an intelligent answer and you call it out and you're *not* right, then she'll bust you. So that's kind of, you know. I've gotten sent down to. . . Mr. S for that, so.

Interviewer: For speaking out without raising your hand?

Jim: For speaking out in class.

Interviewer: And you went into Mr. S and said I'm here because I spoke without raising my hand first.

Jim: Yup! And he made me sign a thing and . . . *That's* a good story I can tell you!

Interviewer: I would love to hear it.

Jim: OK. Well, she called me, this is the third time, the third [warning] she'd given me. Yes, cuz everyone did it. Everyone felt right. She asked for a number. Um, "What is the minimum number of pages you have to do in the essay?" And I said, "Two." And then [I said] like "Five hundred, a thousand, a million." And that's what she doesn't like. And since I was a repeat offender (I thought it was a sensible answer!) I just said, "Two." And then all these other people said, "She kicked you out of class." And I got out there [in the hallway] and I said, "Should I just go down to Mr. S.?" And she said, "Yes." Cuz every time, she kept saying this is the last time, this is the last time, you know? So when I did get kicked out I thought I might as well just straighten it out now. So I went down to Mr. S's office and I sat and I told him what happened and he said, "Well, we're going to figure out an apology." I said, "That's fine. I'll go apologize for it." He said no, I need to be present. And I was like, "OK, that's fine." He's like, "OK, Jim, what are you going to say?" I said, "I'm sorry for calling out in class?" He said, "Wait a second. Here's what we're going to do." So he made me sit in my chair. I felt like the Army: my feet—toes—pointed straight, my back to the chair, my hands on my knees, my head up, looking right in his eyes. And I had to apologize. And he started it off with, it's like, "OK Jim, now I'm going to start off and I'll just let you finish: 'Miss E, I'm sorry for disrupting your class and yelling out. I should have raised my hand.' Now, go on."

Interviewer: Go on?

Jim: Yeah. And he was like, "Now finish it." I said, "Well if I do this it's going to sound rehearsed." He said, "Well it should be rehearsed." I was like, "Well then it's not going to be sincere." He's like, "It doesn't need to be sincere. Just . . ." I was like, "Well, usually, apologies, you know, are sincere." Cause I *was* sorry. She's a great teacher, you know. . . English class is one of my favorite subjects. So I said, No, I wouldn't do it, and he was very upset with me. And so ah . . . you know, I played along and I practiced the apology and everything. And then, the next morning when I came in Mrs. E stood there, or sat next to me, not across from me. She stood, sat, next to me which was very, um, *help*ful. She was . . . laid back and everything and I just apologized to her. Totally unlike what we had practiced. So Mr. S was very upset with me.

Interviewer: Because he was there?

Jim: Because he was standing right there and he was listening to me. It was like . . .

Interviewer: You're "off the script."

Jim (nods): So he spoke with me after that. And he was upset! But Mrs. E said,
  "Well Jim, you get As in my class, so we'll just start over." So.
Interviewer: That was nice.
Jim: Yeah!

Mrs. E and Jim are like the policewoman and offender who silently agree
that the judge is obnoxious and leave the courtroom arm in arm. This admin-
istrator may be in a position to make apologies happen but he is definitely the
out-group person in this little scenario. He is no competition for the steady,
albeit demanding, attention of the formidable Mrs. E., who knows her student
well, and knows he regrets being fresh to her in class. As for Jim, he is convinced Mrs. E has a sincere interest in his class progress. Of the assistant principal, he is only amazed by his inauthenticity. When we think how many
times Jim must have repeated this story (*"It doesn't need to be sincere"*) we
can see that he has had reinforced a certain smug dismissal of administrators.

Students don't have to be in the direct line of fire to feel its heat. They are uniform in their empathic discomfort over seeing a classmate "blacklisted for the
day" if they can't understand the reasons for it (*"It kinda brings the whole class
down."*) What students call the freak-out makes the teachers' moods seem capri-
cious. And students don't like personalities that spontaneously combust any
more than teachers do. For Lynn, a self-possessed hockey cheerleader and var-
sity volleyball player who described herself as average in school, the urge to de-
fend someone who is being "yelled at" unfairly, gets the best of her:

Interviewer: Why wouldn't someone recommend a teacher?
Lynn: Maybe because they didn't enjoy the way their teacher taught, or they're
  too rough on certain people, you know? Like in my English class, my teacher
  doesn't like me at all. I know that for a *fact*. And I probably wouldn't advise
  [recommend] her to any of my friends.
Interviewer: How do you know she doesn't like you? Does she treat you . . .
Lynn: Very different. There's like two people in my class that she kind of singles
  out of the class to yell at, and the rest of them she pretty much praises. One
  time I asked her a question and she yelled at me because I wasn't looking at
  her the whole time that she was talking to me, and that didn't go over very
  well with her. And we've gotten into a few other situations that I don't particularly like. Like that other kid in my class, Todd? I'm really good friends
  with, cuz he's in a lot of my classes. And she was yelling at him for no reason. And I don't know. I just can't stand it when a person's getting yelled at
  and they're just sitting there like, "*Whaaat?*" I sat there and thought, Don't
  say anything. And I did. And I knew it was coming. I knew. Then she turned
  to me and started yelling at me and saying I'm just an "immature 8th grader"
  and Oh, I can name a few hundred other things she's called me, but that's all
  right. So, I don't get along with her very well.

SCHOOL RULES

If you're ever in a jam, here I am. If you're ever so happy you land in jail, I'm your bail."

Cole Porter[12]

***

"I've got a date with Jason on Saturday. We're going to detention."

Overheard in Grade 11

When invited to name rules they would change, most students responded with a why-bother shrug. School rules were made clear to them the day they started, and they recognize futility when they feel it. Students did see the existing rules as ones they can manipulate, with a little luck, to their advantage. Someone once said that industry has yet to invent an efficiency system that human ingenuity could not defeat. In these high schools they studiously affirm this. They will reassure the interviewer earnestly, "I always get my tardies in" (up to the limit that doesn't result in detention), just the way adults would use up all their sick days. They will fake an injury to get out of practice then miraculously recover on game day, copy homework at a furious pace in one class for the one that follows, hold up their answer sheets as they pretend to mull over the next question so that their friends behind them can see the answers, sacrifice fast food money to buy Cliff's Notes, wrap their ankles in elastic bandages to get out of running the mile in gym, schedule all orthodontist appointments for their PE hour, saunter down the corridor pretending to forget they still have a cap or headphones on, or toss their car keys to a friend in the hallway between classes with the anxious plea to "Move my car!" before the overtime policeman tickets them (often, by the way, creating a "Where's-my-car?" panic at 3:30). They have developed a gauge that tells them how many times— somewhere between one and two—they can get away with breaking a rule before the consequences are invoked. Teachers know all this too and their reminder that a rule is in violation gets steadily sterner as the infractions repeat. Where there was resistance to school rules, I found it was limited to the rules about only a few things: loitering in the parking lots (*"You'll be eating a sandwich and they'll kick you out of your car. I mean, it's nuts."*), hats (*"I love wearing a hat. I have probably fifteen hats at home. How come girls can wear 'em?"*), tardies, and being reported to the school by the police when they get a citation for being a "minor in possession" of alcohol.

In this Midwest culture that equates punctuality with high regard for the one waiting, the schools take seriously the training of their charges in this norm. Tardies are punished by Saturday morning detention and it is quite faithfully enforced. Many students (64%)[13] work part-time and carry on, chronically unrefreshed by sleep. The first class of the day suffers perhaps the worst effects of all this after-school working.[14] What students would like are one or two more unpunishable tardies. Their real resentment is aroused when a parent's excuse note doesn't get them off the hook. If a parent *knows* about it, how could it be wrong?

MINORS IN POSSESSION

Carin (grade 11): There's one hard liquor that I've ever liked. That's 'Cisco'? My mom bought it for me for my [last] birthday!
Interviewer: Really.

***

"But an intense classroom experience, as it is connected to his everyday home life, had most definitely touched him, prompted him to look around."

Robert Coles[15]

In practice, a teacher might try to relate the subject material to the student, or at least ask for opinions and reactions to information. He hopes that it matters enough, or connects to the student's experience enough that she will reflect on it. But even the experienced teacher doesn't always expect the full response that a chance mention gets. As the year of this study went on, an amazing number of students I interviewed responded to a prompt card that said "sad" by mentioning alcohol abuse among friends or family. Here the teacher's lesson takes a surprising turn:

English class, late August

The sun bakes the windows of this south side room; the hot Formica desktop can be felt right through my notepaper. The boards have three divisions with head-lines: "assignments," old school play posters and "Junior English" with illus-trations of various authors and characters. New Yorker *magazine covers divide the 3 sections. American flag hangs flat against the wall. The class has been reading* Yellow Raft, Blue Water[16] *for over a week.*

Teacher: Your job is to write an essay of 500 words [as if] you are a Native American teenager living on a reservation. What is your life like? What are your experiences?

Colin to Josh: 500 words? (groans).

Pammi comes in five minutes late.

Mr. D interrupts himself and says to her: I'm talking about the writing of an essay.

Pammi (loudly over her shoulder): OH! OK!

But as she says this, she keeps walking away from him toward the back of the room, the uninterested look on her face not matching the volume of her response.

Teacher (continues): This is a story about growing up female in America. . . Raymona always lived in the shadow of her brother. . . . Metaphorically it is the end of the world . . . it is the End of the World.

Class is silent.

Student (abruptly): On the worksheet do we put one name under each category?
Teacher: Yes.

John reads a book for another class throughout teacher's lecture

Teacher (continues): Females in America . . . poverty . . . alcoholism . . . Who is affected by alcoholism in this book?

Suddenly ten different kids call out a name. Everyone's speaking at once. The class feels like a new place, alive. Only the black male student is silent.

Even John, who has not looked at the teacher because he is reading an assignment for another class, joins the fray by calling out "Foxy" twice, without even looking up from the illicit textbook. The teacher notices his answer the second time:

Teacher: Yes, Foxy.
Who are your favorite characters? (no response.)
Raymona? (no response)
Christine? (no response)
Aunt Ida? (only Colin raises his hand.)
Teacher (nods): In some ways Aunt Ida is the most interesting character in this story."

When Mr. D finishes his lecture, Pammi leaves the room as nonchalantly as she entered, to go to the Learning Disabled (LD) classroom in the basement for help on the essay. Note: The next week Pammi will tap her drowsy neighbor on the shoulder and show her the paper she just got back, 2 or 3 typed pages, with an "A" underlined twice by the grader. Pammi (incredulously): "Do you know how much work I didn't do?" By October this eighteen-year-old junior will quit school to join a boyfriend in Arizona.

Even students noticed that the subject of drinking is so popular it can draw people into classroom conversations who would have nothing in common otherwise:

Scott: Everybody drinks, you know? I'm not really into it, you know, but just to give you an example: in my speech class, it was right in the back corner, it

was, like, me, (and) this guy who kinda fit into the "smokers," this hockey
player, and this other girl. We were just the best friends in that class but we
all had totally different worlds when we left. And so it's, like, in all them three
(sic), you know, they talked about drinking all the time. That's all they did.

Students are drinking at rates that continue to alarm. In North Dakota, the
number of students in grades 9 to 11 who admitted they had drunk alcohol
within the past month was 63% (51% nationally). Of those, 47% (34% nationally) admitted to binge drinking, that is, having more than 5 drinks at one
sitting in the past month.[17] And this trend crosses all student types (*"We have
some honor students who are so into drinking they should be in rehabilitation
. . . some people who are just quiet and shy . . . but they will say, I'm so hung
over I can't see straight."*) Students who want to drink—and there are
many—told me that they have no trouble at all obtaining it: they help themselves to the home supply when "the 'rents" are gone, get older siblings to
buy it for them; get some college-age assistant coaches to buy it for them
(*"One [assistant] coach was really open about drinking and sexual behavior
and stuff. So one guy just asked him and he said sure . . ."*), get themselves invited to university parties by kids who were only a year ahead of them in high
school; steal it as they check in a liquor delivery for their golf club job. They
will wait in a parking lot and ask customers to make a purchase for them (of-
fering a fee for their trouble); gratefully accept cans of beer as a tip for de-
livering pizza to college fraternities; or falsify an ID and present it on request.
And every single one of them will come to know which of the liquor stores,
in and out of town, will let them buy without asking for proof of age.

The sheer amount of unsolicited discussion on the topic of drinking in this
study was notable. I had no direct question on drinking for my interviews but
it came up in response to prompt cards such as, "torn between," "sad,"
"worry" or "strong conviction." Many students described themselves as
"partiers," a euphemism for drinking with their friends. They admitted this in
response to a statement I asked all of them to complete: "What my teachers
do not know about me is . . ." Students' responses presented something of a
paradox: although many, if not most of them admitted to drinking, they believed that—as a major problem that will result in tragedy sooner or later—
adults should be taking a stronger stand against it. Students' resentment about
teacher apathy, or feigned ignorance, in the face of cheating paled next to
their resentment of teachers, coaches and parents who react to students' drinking with a what-can-you-do detachment. (And who could blame them for this
attitude, since rumors persisted about parents who supplied their teens with
beer in the basement "rec rooms" believing that it was better to know where
they were drinking than to have their offspring "sneak around.") Athletes

themselves sounded bitter about stories of someone whose voice was valued for a choral groups's performance, and whose "minor-in-possession" did not disqualify him from *his* activity, singing. Team members who practiced faithfully and kept their training only to be bypassed by the coach on game day were furious about high-performance team members who were discovered drinking and forgiven quietly.

Yet other students did not appreciate the school district rule that requires police to report them to the school, if they have been arrested for possession of alcohol. There is widespread feeling that the rule against merely being at the location or in the vehicle with an open container of beer or liquor should be relaxed. The penalty for everyone is a 6 week suspension from all school activities, essentially finishing various competitions for someone whose mistake was designating himself the safe driver ("*[6 weeks] is a pretty substantial penalty. And for tennis and golf, that's all season. . . You're done, pretty much*"). We recall that students were curious about how teachers perceived them, since they thought grades were influenced by getting on their good side. If students are reported as being in possession of alcohol they felt quite sure the news affected the teachers' treatment of them. They have no chance to explain the circumstances to everyone who knows only of the arrest itself. The fact that the student is then dropped from participating in all school activities for six weeks makes the news even more subject to public discussion.

Krista: I think that the school gets too involved in our personal lives . . . I don't think that when kids get a minor, that the school should really have any impact on it. I mean it just seems like they're trying to take over our lives more so than our parents. You know, they're trying to be our parents. I just don't think that they have any right to our personal lives. That takes the fun out of school.

Interviewer: Do you have friends whose parents found out from the school? Don't they usually find out from the police?

Krista: Oh yeah, they do. But all the teachers find out . . . it also happened to me once.

Interviewer: And did you feel like the teachers treated you differently then?

Krista: Um, some of them. They'll catch you and say [among themselves] ". . . what a bad kid." I'm really close with [the abuse counselor] and I can always talk to her about things. But even she really got on my case for it. She told me I shouldn't be able to go to prom. I got [my citation for drinking] the weekend before prom. And the thing is that I wasn't drinking. I was the designated driver. And *I* got the minor-in-possession. She said to me you will not be going to prom and I'm like, I can't believe you're saying that. And so the school really does affect. . .

Interviewer: The school would not let you go? Or your parents would not let you go.

Krista: No. I did end up going. But the school had *thought* about not letting people with minors go to prom. And I just didn't really believe in that. I didn't
think that was any of their business, what happened outside . . .
Because if you get a minor they suspend you. From six weeks suspension from
any school activities? Any school doings. Um . . . .so it was kinda sad, you
know.
Interviewer: Kids complain to me . . . about the fact that you were trying to be
helpful or whatever, and yet you're getting punished just like everybody else.
Were you designated driver cuz you don't drink?
Krista: Yeah, I usually don't. I'm not saying I never have and I never will, but at
that time I was not drinking. I was sober and . . .
Interviewer: OK. Did your parents find out from [the police]?
Krista: Yeah. They got called down to the police station and had to pick me up
at 12:00 at night. And they weren't happy. I got grounded and got my car
taken away [for] a month. I get my license back on Friday though. Cause now
the court takes it away for 30 days. So, I get my license back then—so I'll be
happy.

A national poll[18] conducted to discover the reasons why adolescents drink,
found that it depended on whom they asked: 87 percent of parents thought
that teenagers drank because of peer pressure. But 79 percent of teens who
drank said they drank "for the high."[19] By their own estimate, students in this
study said 60 to 80% of high schoolers drink at least occasionally (actual percentage in North Dakota is 63%). And confirming the research (though con-
trary to the adult perception) non-drinkers say they are not pressured to join
in; they claim that the pressure was high in junior, not senior high. (*"They
don't even pressure it on me anymore. They just go, Oh, it's Nick, he doesn't
drink . . . just leave him alone;" "At first it excluded me, but now people accept it. At first they thought, he's probably boring . . . now they see me around
school away from the parties and they talk to me"*). By the junior year in high
school kids do not hold it against them if they choose not to drink. After all,
they say, it leaves all the more for them.

Terri: People don't pressure you to drink. Once, you know, you're at the party.
It's just a social get together. And if people aren't drinking, it's no big deal.
You don't have to drink. . . . Just being there . . . that's the hottest thing to do
because you know, there's no one [adult] there. You can just do whatever . . .
there's nothing in town to do anyway. I mean drive around Main [Street]?
How [much] fun's that? You can only go up and down that street so many
times, just driving around then . . . we'll play bowling once in a while. . .we're
out to like 2:00 in the morning cuz you can't even get in there till like 1:00 or
whatever. The funnest thing we go to is the parties. The last ones were set up
just by Madison High people. . . And that last day of school we had a cross

Madison/Jefferson one. And it was great. There were so many people out there [in the country]. I mean people you wouldn't even believe, drinking out there. Our star players, I mean, from every sport were out there, just living it up.

Fran does not drink herself but she will take care of friends when they need it:

Interviewer: If you went—for example, say you went out to the kegger, could you walk around with a coke in your hand?

Fran: I could easily. We'd play quarters and everybody would have a beer and I'd have a coke. And people would ask me, Gosh Fran, are you drunk yet? No, sorry. Yeah, it wasn't a big deal. Because they knew that that's how I felt . . . I mean I used to go to parties where I'd have to wipe the puke off walls because [they] were so drunk, they'd thrown up all over somebody's nice clean house and that isn't going to happen to me. I mean, I've learned to cope with that . . . I had a best friend—this guy I used to date—was sitting in the corner crying because he thought I hated him and another girl was sitting there crying because they were starting to date and she thought I hated her. My boyfriend, the guy I was going out with at the time, was running around (and he was sober too!) was running around outside chasing this girl who was running through mud puddles. It was raining out and it was just . . . it was awful. I've gotten them out of a lot of things. I've gotten them home; I've gotten them in the house. I dated this one guy one time. We went out for like 7 months. And he was a heavy drinker when we started going out. One night we were at a party and he got so drunk he just couldn't get home. And I took him home, I put him in bed and I left him. The next day, I said, Jeremy, if I ever see you drinking again it's over. And for 7 months he didn't drink. But he was to the point of being an alcoholic when we started dating. He was drinking every night . . . quitting jobs left and right and all. Spending too much money. I just don't see drinking to the point of throwing up the next morning and not even remembering what you did the night before and stuff like that.

Two hundred years ago Rousseau (not much of a family man himself, as it happens[20]) wrote that the charms of the home are the best antidote to vice.[21] Today he is still right: researchers have found that the statistic that correlated most significantly with teens' decision to be non-drinkers was their fear of parent reaction.[22] My interviews confirmed this. Many said they were too guilt-ridden ("*I feel really bad the next day, because I let down everyone. My family thinks I'm perfect so I don't do it very often.*"), too anxious ("*What do I worry about? Getting caught at parties. . .*" or too scared ("*If I got caught my dad would just really get mad at me*"). The strict parent still has tremendous sway—if the teen knows she will enforce the consequences ("*My mom said if she caught me, I'd have to tell the team that I couldn't play*").

Athletes who obeyed the rules saw themselves socially marginalized during their season, ("*So I mean during sports and stuff, I don't even think about going out to anything like that. But I usually don't get invited to them any-ways, because they know I'm not gonna drink so"*). Female athletes were pitied because their strict basketball coach will suspend them if they are caught at a party where there is alcohol at any time during the year. This rule definitely restricted their social life as friends pass them over when giving out invitations (*"What's the sense of taking-her-with [sic]? If you want to go to a party you ain't gonna take someone that can't be there"*). A team needs every player to show up clear-headed, so it may not be surprising that a num-ber of athletes wanted tougher penalties for spoiled team mates who cost them a game, or even—according to persistent rumor—a championship (*"All they were thinking about was going out after State [championship games]. The whole time: party."*) They wistfully laid out the "if onlies," advocating a penalty that would keep offenders from playing (*"Cuz lots of 'em love their sport. And if they couldn't play, they might stop drinking;" "[if] you don't care enough about the team, then I don't think that you should be there"*). Whether they have actually earned this reputation or not, the athletes were known for drinking both in and out of their sport's season. It could be that ath-letes who are unpopular taint the reputations of all others (*Cheerleaders and jocks—they're more on the popular side and they can go to college parties cuz they know college people—and they do tend to drink more"*). Or it could be that if they are caught, athletes' disqualifications from playing make their of-fense more widely known than that of someone who does not have a public role in school. Usually fear of competing on the field keeps students from try-ing out for a team. For some, insecurity as a drinker, not player, might keep them from participating:

> Eric: Yeah. I played hockey and JV and stuff in 10th grade and stuff. I didn't play this year. Because um, I don't like a lot of the guys on there that are jerks. And I can't drink as much as they do so . . . I can't really keep up. It's my big prob-lem there. It just that you're kind of apart from the rest of the room. Cause you're not out drinking every weekend. And so I just played hockey out in the park and stuff.

There is an old conservative adage that a law eventually comes to have the opposite effect of its intent. It would be hard to imagine how a rule against drinking would make a teenager drink more, but Jackie proves it. All her life she has been a natural player of many sports. Like Eric (above), her decision not to play basketball is related to drinking. But it's not that she can't keep up with athletes who party. Jackie actually is afraid of her very strict basketball coach, who would eventually kick her off the team for her social life. And then her parents would find out. Jackie opts for the good time. She can fool the "fam" indefinitely, but not the tyrannical coach, Mrs. R:

Jackie: It's just *being* at a party [that gets you in trouble]. But it's so hard. Mrs. R has a rule: if you're caught drinking or caught at a party you get suspended 3 games. With anyone. In a car. Anywhere. If there's alcohol in a car or anything. You get suspended 3 weeks. So that's one of the reasons why I didn't play basketball. Because I hang around a lot of people that go to parties and I knew I'd be off the team anyway and then I'd have to explain it to my parents. What's the point? I mean, I knew I was gonna sit on the bench. Why miss all the parties and not be able to play, have to go to all the practices? It makes no sense! See, P.J., she wants to go to parties. She wants to fit in with everyone else. But basketball means a lot to her. [Players] are pulled from both sides. And if you want to meet a lot of people that's where you gotta go. You gotta go to the parties! That's where you meet everyone.

Students' drinking is not confined to parties in the evenings or at athletic events. Some will return to an empty home or drive someplace in their car, have a drink during their lunch hour and go back to school ("*People in our school, the last couple weeks at school went out and drank at lunch hour or something, then came back*"). It is difficult to estimate how prevalent this practice was, but it happened enough to get several spontaneous mentions in conversations.

Shelly: Well, one time—this just amazed me—other people get away with it all the time. Me, I go out and have one drink. One drink. In the hour and a half, I'm out. Cuz, I have lunch and then free hour right after. One drink. Course, it was a rum and coke. And I come back, after one drink. Then Mrs. F starts ragging on me, Have you been drinking? Shelly, tell me honestly, have you been drinking? I mean, one, I'm not gonna say, "Yeah." You know, knowing that if I [had told the truth], she wouldn't have turned me into the office anyway. But she seemed so concerned! I felt so bad about lying. And I was [already] in trouble. But I still felt bad.

Interviewer: Did she stand close to you then? Is that how. . .

Shelly: I asked her if I could go to the bathroom. She followed me half way down the hall. Then she asked me and I was, like, *No.* I mean, what do you say? You're sitting here; you smell like alcohol. *No.* And you know, [teachers] just believe you fully, too. After that I just . . . that was the first, and last, I ever drank during school hours.

As I observed classes all day, my time coincided with some students more than once in a given day. Alan's behavior in seventh period was so completely different from what I observed hours earlier (8:00), that he sometimes seemed like two entirely different people. On this day he was completely gregarious at 2:30 in the afternoon, face flushed, loud, and indiscreet. Alan told me in his interview that since the death of a relative that year he had seen his grades

slide from all A's to D's. He said that he only drank on weekends, but his behavior would make one wonder:

English Class, February

Class is very noisy; it's the last period of the day.

> *A boy and a girl stare at each other from across the room.*

Girl (sarcastically): I love you too, Mike.
Boy to her: Too bad I have no response.
Girl: Huh?
Boy: Too bad I have no response
Girl: You have no what?
Boy: Response. Response. I have No Response.

> *The boy from chemistry, Alan, who was working alone and silently this morn-*
> *ing and never speaks to me or anyone there, is also in this class. When he sees*
> *me he suddenly says loudly, as if startled, "Whooaa, we're in three classes*
> *together."*

Class will not settle down.

Teacher: You people act crazy just because we have a guest.

> *She looks down at me at the end of the room. "We're not like this usually."*
> *Three times she says, "We're not like this." I finally say, "I believe you."*

Alan: She's always here, she's in my first period (and to me he says something
like "you really otta get a life" but he's very friendly).
Teacher: Why do you act like first graders when you're 11th graders?
Alan (to teacher): You're blushing.
Teacher: Well, I'm upset. Why do you act this way?
The teacher is at the front of the room, maybe ten feet from him yet Alan starts
talking to many people at once.
Alan: I'm having three keggers, one for (inaudible: Valentine's Day?), one for
(inaudible: St. Patrick's Day?) and one tonight.
Boy (glances quickly at the front of the room to see if teacher is listening): Oh,
you mean we're meeting at the Kegs (a hamburger stand), right?
Alan: Yeah, yeah right, we're meeting at the Kegs.

> *Teacher shows no sign of hearing any of this.*

Girl (to Alan): Last night I was really blind.
Alan: Oh, you didn't have that much.
Alan (to same girl): I went from a 52 to a 94 in one day. . . I complained.
Girl: How did you do it?
Alan: Well, I had not done the assignment but I passed in all my homework late
and did a little "extra work."
Girl: You can bullshit.

Alan: Yeah, I can bullshit.

Commotion continues. Teacher seems exasperated.

Teacher: Take a clean piece of paper. This is not a quiz. What is it that Huck Finn says?

People look at her blankly.

Teacher: What is it that you individually could do to improve your group's discussion?

Alan: Join a psychology group.

Teacher puts them in working groups of three and four. Some of them turn their desks; some hardly bother to change at all.

Alan: Can we answer these questions as a group?

Teacher: No, individually.

Teacher's moving around among the groups.

Teacher (to boy): What are you doing?

boy (very emphatically): Answering the questions!

Teacher: Good. Turn your chair around so you can share your answers.

The boy shakes his head in disbelief, sighing as if to say, Nothing I do is right.

Teacher: No, no, that's good. I'm glad you're answering. Just turn your chair around.

Students have nominated someone to go to the front of the room, put their answers on the overhead and share them with the rest of the class. So one by one they have a chance to be teacher for five minutes. Usually the person doing the reporting is not the same person who wrote it down. When Alan, the kegger-organizer, is up there he has a hard time focusing the overhead and the class moans and groans that they can't see.

Alan: Ah, shut up.

Teacher: Alan.

Alan: I should've brought my sunglasses. I can't see my notes from here so I can't discuss my answers.

He becomes increasingly sarcastic as he reads the answers from his group.

Alan (as he finishes lesson): Where's my standing O?

Teacher: OK, who's next?

No group moves.

Alan (loudly, back in his seat): Come on, you wimps.

Teacher (quietly to the class): Some of his comments aren't necessary but that's all right.

By the end of the year Alan's rude and boisterous behavior (also described in Chapter 3) has become too much for Mrs. F and she expels him from what she has told me is one of the brightest classes she's ever had. Another student describes Alan as "brilliant" in chemistry. But for the last week of the year, he spends five straight English periods in the assistant principal's office. In an interview Alan responds to the prompt word, angry:

> Alan: Angry? I have to say um, the faculty at school here and my parents. I get angry at all the pressure that they put on me. See I have an older brother and, he's not smart. He got B's, well he mainly got C's. You know, they'd say, "Oh great job! You got a B in this class." I'd come home from school with one B and I'd get yelled at, "Why did you get a B in this?" It's not so much my mom as my dad. The pressure really got to me. And like Mr. M. which I personally hate always, whenever he brings me into the office, like the last time I was there, I walked in there, there's some guy in there. And Mr. M. said, "Oh, well, since you're here, let's bring up Alan's file and I'll show you my file [sic]." You know, why is he showing this guy, that I don't even know, my file? And I found out later that it was the new vice principal, the one that's starting next year, so then I wasn't as upset. But you know, don't ask for my permission or anything (sarcastically). Maybe I didn't want it brought up at that particular moment! But he brings it up and he says "Well, you see Alan has, has very good potential. He's in all AP classes here." And then he says, "But he's a trouble maker." He said, "He has trouble keeping his mouth shut." And I was ready to leave, to keep my mouth shut and kind of shut the door behind me at the same time. That would have just made things even worse.

NOTES

1. Whitehead, Alfred North (1948/1974), *Science and Philosophy*, NY: Philosophical Library, p.45.

2. "Americans have disengaged psychologically from politics and government [from 1973 to 1993]. The proportion of Americans who reply that they trust their government in Washington 'only some of the time' or 'almost never' has risen steadily from 30 percent in 1966 to 75 percent in 1992," in: Putnam, Robert D. (1995), "Bowling Alone: America's Declining Social Capital," *Journal of Democracy, 6, 1*, 65–78.

3. Swanson, Dena Phillips, Margaret Beale Spencer, and Anne Petersen (1998), "Identity Formation in Adolescence," *The Adolescent Years: Social Influences and Educational Challenges: Ninety-seventh Yearbook of the National Society for the Study of Education*, Chicago: University of Chicago Press.

4. Perry, William, C. (1968), *Forms of Intellectual and Ethical Development in the College Years: A Scheme*, NY: Holt, Rinehart and Winston.

5. "But the solicitation of student views is often followed by an authorized teacher "truth," which so often derives from the pressures of standardized testing which render students' views basically irrelevant to education. Pedagogies that invite

participation, but then ignore it, are obvious when a teacher, following an intense and complex discussion, reverts to old notes or those written on the blackboard, demanding that they be transcribed into student notebooks," in Fine, Michelle (1991), *Reframing Dropouts: Notes on the Politics of an Urban Public High School*, Albany: SUNY Press, p.45.

6. Knowles, John (1959), *A Separate Peace*, NY: Bantam, p.18.

7. Cusick, Philip (1973), *Inside High School: The Student's World*, NY: Holt, Rinehart and Winston, p.175.

8. Cormier, Robert (1974), *The Chocolate War*, NY: Doubleday, p.166.

9. Burling, Robbins (1970), *Man's Many Voices: Language in Its Cultural Context*, NY: Holt Rinehart & Winston; Hymes, Dell (1974), *Foundations in Sociolinguistics: An Ethnographic Approach*, Philadelphia: University of Pennsylvania Press.

10. "The discourse that a group of like-minded people uses defines the community and its product as well," in Berkenkotter, Carol, Thomas Huckins and John Ackerman (1989), "Social Context and Socially Constructed Texts: The Initiation of a Graduate Student into a Writing Research Community," Berkeley: Center for the Study of Writing, Technical Report No. 33.

11. For a comparison of a self-effacing teacher with a teacher who is not, see Mohatt, Gerald, and Frederick Erickson (1981), "Cultural Differences in Teaching Styles in an Ojibwa School: A Socio-Linguistic Approach," in Trueba, H., G.P. Guthrie and C. Au, eds. (1981), *Culture and the Bilingual Classroom: Studies in Classroom Ethnography*, Rowley: Newbury House.

12. "Friendship," by Cole Porter © 1939 (Renewed) Chappell & Co. All Rights Reserved. Used by Permission. Warner Bros. Publications U.S., Inc., Miami, Florida, 33014.

13. In North Dakota 64% of all high school students are employed: 22% work 10 hours or less per week; 25% work 11–20 hours; 15% work 21–40 hours, and 1.6% work over 40 hours. Source: North Dakota Risk Behavior Survey, North Dakota Dept. of Public Instruction, 1997.

14. Dement, William C. (1999), *The Promise of Sleep*, NY: Delecorte Press.

15. Coles, Robert (1989), *The Call of Stories: Teaching and the Moral Imagination*, Boston: Houghton Mifflin, p. 27.

16. Dorris, Michael (1987), *Yellow Raft, Blue Water*, NY: H. Holt.

17. North Dakota residents rely more on private transportation than public, which impacts driving statistics: 37% (17% nationally) of North Dakota students in grades 9–12 admit to drinking and driving. Source: North Dakota Risk Behavior Survey, North Dakota Dept. of Public Instruction, 1997.

18. A Hazelton Foundation (Center City, MN) study found that peer pressure to drink is less than parents think: "87% of parents said teens drink or use drugs because everyone else is doing it but 79% of teens said they indulge simply because they like the feeling of being high." See "Generations split on chemical abuse: Report finds parents, teens don't share views on alcohol, drug abuse," in *The Star Tribune*, Minneapolis, Oct., 1995, p.3.

19. Only 19% of students reported feeling "pressured" to use drugs or alcohol: Shell Poll (1999).

20. Smith, L. Glenn and Joan K. Smith (1994), *Lives in Education: A Narrative of People and Ideas* (2nd ed.), NY: St.Martin's, p.163.

21. Rousseau, Jean-Jacques (1911/1969), *Emile*, translated by Barbara Foxley. Everyman's Library: NY: Dutton; London: Dent, p.13.

22. Teens who get "a lot" of parental warnings report using drugs at a lower rate (26%) than those teens who "never" get parental warnings (37%). PRIDE Survey (1997), Atlanta: National Parents Resource Institute for Drug Education.

Chapter Three

Bothered

". . . It seems like the classes got harder in ninth grade and they started to hurt more."

Angie, Grade 11

***

"If someone asked me what my address was when I was seven years old, the numbers wouldn't flash before my eyes. I'd have to relive a specific moment: the heat of the day, the smell of the cut lawn, the slap-slap-slap of rubber thongs against my heels. Then once again I'd be walking up the two steps of the poured concrete porch, reaching into the black mailbox, heart pounding, fingers grasping — Where is it? Where's that stupid letter from Art Linkletter, inviting me to be on his show? But I wouldn't give up hope. I'd think to myself, Maybe I'm at the wrong address. But no, there they are, the brass numbers above, 3-6-2-4, complete with tarnish and rust around the screws. That's what I remember most, not addresses, but pain."

Amy Tan[1]

Students' language to describe what bothers them about school is notable for its mechanistic, even painful metaphors. Jim says, "I'd open [my geometry book] up and my mind would just shut down." Several complained that teachers try to "drive it into you." They see their minds as miniature warehouses, objecting that teachers, "try to pack all this information in you, and there's not enough room!" Others might be Dickensian orphans: "I don't like it when they beat it into your head." Such paranoia can shape the rest of the school experience: one state-ranked athlete trained vigorously for his three sports' seasons "to get away from teachers, always beatin' down your neck."

Nate's state of mind when he is taking an exam shows how annoying a common enough classroom situation, a multiple-choice test, can be:

> Nate: Just [kids'] talking . . . annoys me. We just had our final and I thought I was doing well. Part of [the final] was matching. A big matching. And I was just like Oh, this could go there and there and I just got all frustrated and I just felt like screaming and ripping my hair in my head. And this kid, he's sort of talking behind me and I just turned on him. . . I gave him one evil look. I just felt like going over there, [and saying], "Just Shut Up!"

How does it happen that a seemingly normal student will entertain thoughts of violent acts in a school setting? (We could make more sense of them if they were sense*less* acts among strangers in a train station.) Had he endured a series of social, parental, evaluative or administrative (but above all, social) indignities and finally reached the end of his patience? Here Tanya, who in effect, worked three hours at her fast food job to pay the overdue fine, is furious at an administrative "wrong." It happens in that soundless center of flat affect, the library. We are grateful for the school's "zero tolerance" for weapons:

> Tanya: This library. They keep saying that I have overdue magazines and stuff? I've gotten pegged for 2 magazines. I had to pay for 2 of em! That I turned *in*. I was so mad. You know, they don't give you your *report card* if you don't . . . And I'm like . . . I had to pay for em! And I know I brought em back in. Oh, that made me so mad. And just like, about a month ago — You know the history report I was talking about? I turn my book in. Three weeks later I get an overdue book notice. I was so mad. Right there, I went up. Like, I'm on a rampage. I went straight down here and I'm just ready to freak. I'm like. . ." I brought this book in about a month ago, could you check this again?" And I'm just waiting for her to go . . . you know, "We're holding it." And then the lady walks over there and picks it out of the shelf. And she's like, "Oh here it is. Yeah. Sorry about that." I'm like, Take this piece of paper and get out of my face. I just had that happen to me *twice*. Cuz, it said if you don't get it in your *report card* will be held. I'm like, *I'm gonna shoot somebody in the school*. Get on the ball here! I turned it in, like, 3 weeks before! It's like . . . get a *brain* here!

Most students do not come anywhere close to perpetrating violence in school[2] but there is no denying that many feel quite "bothered" a few times in a given day (*"It was the daily work that killed me."*) It is a distracting feeling one girl calls the "ningee bingees," an aggravated, sinking, disconnected state of mind, different from the old feeling of being coerced.

I myself felt unseen during my nine months of observation. As a non-participant observer, I wanted to be unseen. But I was not different from all the other "disconnected" students I sat with in the back of the room. We were all, essentially, unseen. I suppose I was entitled to get up and leave, get a drink, stroll around for some exercise, make a phone call, drop in on the friendly principal, chat with a teacher friend during her prep period. I did not do any of these things because it seemed impolite to the teacher whose class I was observing. Besides, the purpose of my research was to rediscover what it was like to go to school all day long. Giving in to my inclination to move around after a few hours would have defeated this goal. And though it was research I chose for myself, sitting in classes I felt restricted a lot of the time. I felt, actually, disenfranchised, as though I had no vote in any of what transpired there. I was very aware of a tone of condescension, vague disappointment or outright exasperation that I heard many tired teachers use during the day to their classes. Often teachers resort to a sarcasm they would never use with adults; and it almost never gets a chuckle from the class. By 11 A.M. I was exasperated at the thought that I had four and a half more hours to go. By 3:30, virtually no one had spoken to me by name, no one had asked me how I was, no one noticed that I was perhaps furious, weepy, or on the edge of violent or suicidal behavior. I was none of these things—but I could have been. Any of the people sitting around me could have been. And no one noticed because the crowds and pace of the day make it impossible to do so. I thought: this is what it feels like to be friendless, or clique-less in school. It was a feeling of isolation so unnatural to me that I would not choose to do all-day classroom research again. And this was despite the fact that I was learning something about adolescents that fascinated me! What of kids who have no interest in what the teacher is saying? How can they bear the feeling of dry disconnection from topic and people? (Her elementary teachers used to suggest at parent conferences that my daughter liked to "visit" in school a bit too much. The teacher in me felt apologetic at the time, but now I see that connecting to friends is what makes school feel alive.)

BORED

"I've never done a history assignment cuz I hate reading about it—it's even worse than listening to it."

Gordon, Grade 11

***

"As I inched sluggishly along the treadmill of the Maycomb County school system, I could not help receiving the impression that I was being cheated out of something. Of what I knew not, yet I did not believe that twelve years of unrelieved boredom was what the state had in mind for me."

Harper Lee[3]

By far the biggest complaint students had about school is that it is boring. School has always been something of a weak competitor for the student's attention. It was more fun in the nineteenth century to go fishing than to sit with your *McGuffey Reader*,[4] and kids' natural desire to move and breathe outside with pals certainly has not changed in a hundred years. The early twenty first century however, brings a different quality of distraction. Now not only fishing friends, but lovers, jobs, television, movies, video games, computers, e-mail, magazines, pulp fiction, birth control choices, abortion decisions, alcohol, drugs, music videos, cd's, rock concerts, fashion dictates, tattoos, body piercing, hair dyeing, transferred families, divorcing parents, menacing teachers, meddling principals, overbearing coaches, moody directors, aggressive college recruiters, insensitive employers and exotic extra-curriculars all crowd noisily in, clamoring to have the student look them over. What is more, television has habituated children's attention span to something less than two minutes. Early Childhood educators are the first professionals to face kids who, by five years old, are used to zippy animation and simple plot solutions.[5] School is drearily different: plodding, yet complicated. So after parents have abandoned their kids on a wide, pre-school court of unsupervised television, teachers file grimly on to play a twelve-year, catch-up game: down a few points as they enter every period.

At the very beginning, youngsters are fascinated by the newness of school, even its constraints (*"Kenny laid down on the floor, and Mrs. Morris told him to Get In His Seat," reports the wide-eyed kindergartner*). Later, as they leave the primary grades behind, children will begin to answer flatly, Ok*ay*, to the trite old question, How's school? What have changed are the role of the teacher, and the teacher's expectations of the students. Pedantry and ceaseless evaluation have begun to define the experience more and more. We learn that students spend the largest share of their time listening, writing in workbooks, and waiting: 76% of the time in class is spent on instruction, 20% on class routines and 2% on activity. In less than one percent of the cases are students asked to respond in any way that require reasoning or shaping of meanings.[6]

Students certainly did not hold back when describing "teacher telling," as drab and dull. In a popular "Far Side"[7] cartoon the dog owner is leaning over the dog in the first frame, scolding, "Okay, Ginger! I've had it! You stay out of the garbage! Understand, Ginger? Stay out of the garbarge, or else!" Above we read, "What we say to dogs." In the next frame the owner is leaning over the dog scolding, "Blah blah Ginger blah blah blah blah blah blah blah blah blah blah blah blah blah Ginger blah blah blah blah blah blah blah blah . . ."

Above it says, "What they hear." When the topic is of little interest to her, the student becomes like Ginger, unable to hear a single instruction. Asked to describe a class they do poorly in, they quickly cite the teacher's "babbling," or "mumbling on." "He's just up there rattling."

> Lonny: But when he just sits there and blah blah blah?—that's about what I hear! When he just sits there and just explains it? How to do something? Like, give me a logical use for it and then sit and listen to you but otherwise I'll doze off or read a book.

It is hard to imagine how we could accomplish teaching without speaking, sophisticated software notwithstanding. But to many students the problem with school is the relentless sound of the teacher's voice. The worst review one student can give another about a teacher is: "Every day is the whole hour of him talking." The practical among them might take the chance to write notes or do other homework. The below-average student will get discouraged by the complexity and give up (*"He lectures . . . but I was just lost and I'm like, not. So I didn't take any more [notes]"*). Even the brightest students can have their problems with teacher-talk (*"I'll read the chapter; I understand it. And then he'll have to explain it for two days in class!"*) The teacher's voice even has the effect of making routine seat work seem more interesting by comparison (*"He sits there and talks and talks and talks. I finally just start on the workbook—so I don't fall asleep;"*) or other pieces of curriculum more appealing (*"It was great when we got to watch movies cause he wouldn't sit there and talk"*). Their friends will nod with empathy, knowing that the videos mean at least a chance to daydream, if not "power nap." When the lecture gets too far from their interests, the students in the back will share their stories in whispers:

English class, September

Mr. N distributes vocabulary sheets on which students have written, using words in a sentence; also distributes the assigned "Letter written to the curriculum committee" to ask that Native American literature be included.

Teacher: Put an asterisk on your paper and return it and I'll review it, if you want me to reconsider your grade.

He gives out papers and passes around the stapler as public address comes on: ". . . set construction for Music Man . . . first meeting tomorrow night . . . first read-through today at 3:45."

Teacher (goes over grades): A means you . . . B means you . . . and rationalized pretty well. C means you did well but you offered no rationalization for the Native American curriculum in your letter . . . (begins lecture): John Smith's letters to England [said] . . . anyone can do it here . . . I was surrounded by about twenty natives in the woods and I beat them all . . .

Addie: (in low voice to girls sitting around her, who stare front as they listen):
She was drunk and she puts her arms around Sean.
Girls: Sean who?
Addie: My Sean! So I'm, like, OK, uh, fuck off!
Teacher (ignores the muffled undertone of girls' conversation: The implication is
that you too can beat them . . . he lied about the climate, the hardship . . . half
of them died the first winter. . .black men were inferior (sarcastically), you
know, hellions too . . . Pocahontas came upon them torturing John Smith. She
was so taken with his looks, the white man, his physique, she had never seen
anything like that before . . . she threw herself on him to save him.

As Mr. N says, She threw herself on him, the sleeping student in the last row slaps
his eyes open. Girl cleans her ring with a safety pin as teacher tells the Poc-
ahontas story. When he says, Pocahontas was enthralled with the look of the
white man, she turns, frowns at her friends, and raises her shoulders with a
tiny head-shake of amused puzzlement, as if to say, What's the big deal?

Teacher talk is not the only factor contributing to the flat energy level in
school There's no doubt that the environment of some classrooms, the time of
the day and old, ingrained learning habits contribute to the feeling of being
lulled to sleep:

Angie: [Math] is boring. He talks all the time. . . . You practically fall asleep:there's
no windows in that class. It drives me nuts. It's darker in there. It's like we're just
locked in this room. And you try and understand it and you can't, I just can't understand it! And he's doing all this stuff, even if I ask him a question and stuff I
still don't understand it. I'm not good in math and science. Science is different.
Science is a big old room with plants: you could breathe. But in math, it's like
you're locked in a hole and you can't wait for the time to go by. Every five minutes I'm looking at the clock and it goes so slow and it's like, next hour's lunch
and your stomach's starting to growl and you're getting hungry and you can't
wait to get out of that class. Towards the end of the hour we can talk to friends,
but pretty much he sits and talks the whole hour. It's sorta like my English
teacher, he talks all the time. I'd like him to give us time to work.

Dianne Ackerman claims that we honestly come by our need for novelty,
that it derives from our ancestors' habituation to a survival mode that served
them well:

A constant state—even of excitement—in time becomes tedious, fades into the
background, because our senses have evolved to report changes, what's new,
something startling that has to be appraised: a morsel to eat, a sudden danger.
. . So it is not only possible but inevitable that a person will grow used to a
city's noises and visual commotion and not register these stimuli constantly.
On the other hand, novelty itself will always rivet one's attention.[8]

Students will create their own novelties to rivet the attention of their friends at every opportunity during their six hours together. After I spent month after month sitting in the back of the class, I cannot say I blamed them. It is absolutely verboten of course, to decide to walk around if your back starts to hurt or you begin to feel just plain anxious from the sameness of the day, hour after hour. What can an energetic adolescent do when the feeling of confinement begins to crowd out logical thought? Friends save the day, says Jenny, "They get some of your jitterness out, from sitting in the class. Friends are a great stress reliever!" Of course, the stress-relieving antics of a friend might actually cause stress in the teacher. It is a trade off the students are willing, if not happy, to make. (This may have been the one time a teacher actually raised his voice in a class I observed.):

Accounting Class, December
There's a big sign, a poster on the wall of this classroom. "What I want to be when I get out of school: rich" and the graphic accompanying this shows a big pile of money. There are 28 kids in this class in five rows sitting elbow to elbow—hardly a place to be had. I squeeze in at the back of the last row in the corner. The room is dim, the shades are drawn. Mr. O comes in and put the light out. The overhead screen is illuminated. It's impossible to see what's on the screen from the last row. I ask the student next to me if she can see it and she says, Just barely.
Teacher (referring to some work he's given them): Do it yourself; it's the only way you'll learn.
Student: Isn't it better to keep it and finish it than pass it in incomplete?"
Teacher: No, pass it in.

He starts a lesson and asks a question. There's no response from the class.

Teacher (sarcastically): This is the class participation section of our class so people can join in. . . What do we do in the case of this problem?

Not a sound. Finally a boy in the middle of the last row, who's been rubbing his cheeks with the palms of his hands, his eyes closed, shouts out, "Increase!" (meaning increase debt).

Teacher: All right Shelby! I thought you were sleeping there for awhile but I guess not.
Shelby punches the air in victory. Suddenly there's a flash of light on the floor. Students shriek. A boy stamps his foot. He had stuck his pen into the flexible electric socket that is sticking up like a single weed in the middle of the floor. In a split second his foot obscures the evidence so that at first the teacher can't see exactly what went on. Mr. O looks over at the commotion, and turns back to the overhead machine. He takes a few moments without looking up, then looks over his glasses straight at the student whose complicit shoe still covers the culprit pen.
Teacher (very sternly): DON'T DO THAT AGAIN. I'M RESPONSIBLE FOR YOUR SAFETY IN HERE. DON'T DO THAT.

Students giggle for the next five minutes as they whisper to each other about what the boy had done. Teacher resumes a long lesson using the overhead. The class is very dim and warm. People eventually get drowsy.

ANGRY

"Forty below keeps the riffraff out."

North Dakota saying

***

"Geography is half of character."

Alfred North Whitehead[9]

This part of the country is most famous for its cold weather, but it is most proud of its status as a place where, by comparison to anywhere else, crime is rare. Six months of below freezing will put the crimp on roving bands of marauding youth. Severe winters and a relatively undiversified economy keep in-migration low. As a consequence the culture is rather homogeneous,[10] that is, one where norms are broadly shared. In a homogeneous culture, communication, even among strangers, is easily accomplished (although not, in this case, voluble). A feeling that we're all in this—often climate-related issue—together, keeps the community blandly cohesive. Witnessing a violation of a strong group norm such as civility feels like watching a small crime against a second cousin. Perhaps because of a tradition of occasionally needing one's "cousins" to get the sandbags in or the sugar beets out (or more likely because small social groups do not tolerate chronic, deep rancor well), a certain relentless courtesy characterizes the personality of the people here. But you can be polite and still be judgmental. And most teenagers' judgments are based on appearance.

The names designating informal student groups in these three schools are vividly diverse: Granolas, Hippies, Hippy-Wanna-Be's (*"blue crappy clothing"*), Ditses, Ditsoes, Socials (*"they never sit alone"*), Party-More People, Preps (*"they always dress up for school"*), Populars, In-People, Snobs (*"bow down, kiss my feet"*), Snobby-richies, Jocks, Weirdoes, Goons, Skaters, Skateboarders (*"have, you know, a skateboarder haircut"*), Burnouts, Grungies (*"they just look cruddy"*), Ditch-School-Type People, Not-Really-Care-People, Smokers, Headbangers, Bangers, Potheads, Motor-Heads (*"black, crappy clothing"*), Metalheads (*"bought all their clothes at a rummage sale"*), Theater Jocks, Drama People, Band Fags, Band Nerds, The Y'know: What-The-Hell-Is-*He*-Doin'-In-Band-People, Towners, Basers, Soaks,

Loads, BOA's (Burnt-On-Arrivals), Loners, Brains, Nerds, Dorks, Geeks, Rejects, Morons, Squeebs, Deebs, and my own personal favorite, The Innocent-Stander-Byers.

Individual students will claim to have a live-and-let-live attitude towards these groups, at least towards those in the lower echelons of the social hierarchy.[11] For one thing, most people are hard to categorize permanently; high school students might change looks and loyalties more than once in three or four years. Many students reported that others changed since they knew them in junior high school, but they figure change is inexorable (*"What kids don't know yet when they start high school is that people they thought they knew, they don't know anymore."*) so they forgive each other for it. Maybe they've changed themselves. And a wealth of school activities assures a certain cross-registration, so to speak, of type. The school that can afford a rich extra-curricular menu will see its students sitting all over the lunchroom. Teams, clubs, societies, choruses, casts, orchestras, bands, yearbook and newspaper staffs have to recruit talent broadly—and tolerate variance in dress, politics and maturity—if they are to succeed (*"In choir there's basically a person from every little clique . . . you're all equalized in there!"*) Pulling together for the win, the fundraising, or the next edition goes a long way towards mitigating the effects of obvious difference. What is more, old sports' and performing arts' friendships from elementary and junior high, and new high school romances that cross town might help slow the rushes to judgment about a rival school. Still, disaffected students who do not share any curricular or extra-curricular interests within a school will draw sharp inferences about what it is those different-looking people believe to be important. In the confined space of a high school building, with a strict reward system, such lack of relatedness can escalate into strained apprehensions and jealousies (*"Not everybody is accepted by everybody else"*). And in a long day with minimum acknowledgment of one's very existence, strained apprehensions can be downright dangerous. If teachers were the source of the frustration over being bored in school, students' peers were the source of their anger (*"Cliques, that's what I hate about this place"*).

Although the Prep group of students dismissed everybody else, the Grungies et al, did not return the favor of indifference. Generally speaking, Grungies resented a clique whose foundation seems to be the expensive label on their clothes. We recall that students think that teachers reward their pets with good grades. Many also believed that the students who are favored by teachers earn their good graces by virtue of a certain "look." It is impossible to overestimate the resentment among students towards others who get more of whatever it is that makes school palatable, just because of the way they dress (*"They have money and they dress just right"*). The attire translates into a perceived status (*"You probably could tell that they were the more popular people if you saw them, just by the way they dress."*) The definition of the group name "Prep" was that they put an effort into their look (*"Hair has to be perfect; they have to have make up just piled on. They have to have just the perfect earrings, perfect clothes."*) Many students indifferently called themselves Preps (*"It's a style of clothes. I'm a Prep."*) Basically it contrasted with every other type of dress in school, and it took the largest budget to accomplish. One student did her own controlled experiment to prove the appeal of "good" clothes:

> Candy: I don't see how people can sit there and say I like you because you wear "Guess" clothes. OK, one day, I wore, like, a designer outfit, and I found a lot more people talked to me then when I was wearing like regular clothes.
> Interviewer: You're kidding.
> Candy: No, it's . . . it's just really strange. I'm like, wait a minute. . . . Some people I haven't even met before were talking to me and stuff and I mean, I talk to everybody.
> Interviewer: So did it make you want to wear designer outfits everyday?
> Candy: Not really, no. I don't want people to like me for the clothes I wear. I don't want people to like me for what I look like. I just want people to like me for me. Because you can't really call them friends if they don't like you for who you are, [if they only] like what kind of money you have or whatever.

In a strange sociolinguistic twist, being named a "popular person" was actually not an attractive designation (*"They are a bit more on the ruder side just because they are the more popular"*). If you were popular, you never applied the term to yourself. If someone used the term about you it would be said derisively, being actually synonymous with "Snob" or "Social." The members of these cliques are said to have a "need to be worshipped," as they "scrape their nose on the ceiling every day." "Snobs" were popular people who had an attitude that was arrogant (*"[Snobs act as though] 'I'm perfect. I'm better than you'"*) or at least insensitive (*"In the hallway they won't say hi back"*). "Socials" were popular people who talked a lot, surrounded by friends, eating in a crowd, always planning, or being apprised of plans for, a party. Socials, who as a category overlapped generously with the Preps as well as with the dreaded teacher's pets, engendered a great resentment in the rank and file (*"I think they're real bitches, excuse my language"*) because they were believed to be able to disregard rules, especially drinking rules at will (*"They act perfect in school but then they just go out and get totally plastered on the weekends"*).

Brent, confiding that his temper is something to contend with on any day, this day is still furious at a classmate who committed two sins: he was "popular" and a liar. We recall the danger to the inept librarian:

Interviewer: What kind of things would set (your temper) off?

Brent: I don't know. Something somebody said about someone else that I know. Happened in the past. Recently. No names on that one. It's one of those angers that you feel like beating the person in front of you and I mean, you can picture yourself actually killing the person. Ripping them to shreds, little by little. It's somebody who is trying to be a dick or something. It's just certain people out there that try to be, you know, the cool ones. Sometimes they consider themselves to be popular kids. They might be popular in that many people *know* 'em. But the majority of people hate their guts.

The fury of these words gets our attention, especially when we consider that in these three schools the atmosphere is quiet, clean, respectable. If a violent incident occurred there people would say that they never thought it could happen in their school.[12] But if adults in charge talked to individual kids—and if they had a genuine level of trust between them—they would learn that even in a predictable school, a few students are walking around with an anger that is as scary as it is hidden. Consider John, a military "brat" who has lived many places, is proud of his straight A average and has hopes for a military career that will begin with admission to the Air Force Academy. His shaved head with its tiny ponytail in back, army boots and love of skateboarding sets him apart from the style of the Preps. Like many of his classmates John begins by telling me that he knows stereotyping is wrong. Nevertheless, his resentment over Preps' stereotyping of *him*, makes him respond in kind:

John: I hate hockey players. I guess they're just kinda, like, the vocational ed people: they have no brain. There's a couple of 'em that are pretty cool, just, like, in all, all places, there's a couple of guys that are pretty cool and like, there's, there's J.B., he's a pretty good friend. He's a hockey player. But, how would you say it without cussing? Well I guess: conceited. They all think they're better. They try to be Preps and they try to be cool and they're not. I mean, if there's like a retarded kid they'll sit there and laugh at him and make fun in front of him, in front of his face. I think that's pathetic. A lot of em try and make fun of my hair. I don't care. I laugh at 'em back. I just say something like, Get original. Like, I don't care! What they think is, you're just a *punk* or a Headbanger. . . . There's a couple of black guys anyway that I like and I'm good friends with, but most of 'em I truly cannot stand and I would like to take a baseball bat to 'em. They're just, cuz they just think they're something they're not. They think they're great. I have nothing against athletes; it's just if they would treat people with a little more respect than they do. And I hate that [rap] music. It irritates me. They'll bring a radio on the bus and they'll play it out loud so everybody can sit back there and hate it. A lot of my friends hate it. It just gets annoying. I mean, how can you appreciate something that's pure cussing? I don't know. So degrading towards most every single thing, like women.

Interviewer: Yeah. I can't wait till that era passes.

Which psycho-social conditions keep John from picking up a baseball bat to the students he despises, and which others have two students execute a nefarious plan to assassinate classmates are not the focus of this discussion. All attended schools that were considered fine, and came from homes presumed "good." Of this much we are sure: we had little idea of the depth of the resentment they harbored towards people different from themselves, especially those in the upper echelons of the student hierarchy, which often has athletes at the top. The differences were based on appearance; and personality characteristics were attributed to appearance that were extremely prejudicial. The apparel of kids in high schools does not have to include black trench coats for it to engender resentment or fear. (The case for school uniforms looks tighter to me all the time.[13] But when I have told adolescents I wore a school uniform, indifferently, for twelve years, they look at me with shock that I came out of it with any personality left.)

Perhaps because their successes are public ones — garnering newspaper notice as well as corridor congratulations — it was the athletes or the cheerleaders who were perceived as believing themselves to be better than others (*"Cuz hockey players here, they rule the school. And the cheerleaders—some of those people really feel that they're on this pedestal way higher than everybody else"*). I would suggest that coaches might rethink the custom of having athletes and cheerleaders dress in a suit and tie, or in their uniforms, on game day. Presumably, this different dress prompts well-wishers to urge good luck on them, over and over; and it reminds fans to show up later that day to support them. It also serves to focus their own attention on the upcoming game. But this custom has another effect: some students resent the unique status conferred by adults on these students (*"Hockey players and basketball players are usually the same ones who give you hell and just are dicks and stuff . . . why go [to a game] and clap for them?"*) If they made honor roll students wear *gold* jackets every day, the hue and cry from the parents of B, C and D students would drown out a pep band. Choice of style is an extremely powerful mode of communicating who it is an adolescent believes himself to be. When they dress up on game day, athletes and cheerleaders are communicating not merely a difference but a specialness. Fairly or not, this gets interpreted as conceit. (It doesn't help that they are excused so often from the same test schedule as everybody else, at least in a state where teams often travel for hours to play their opponents.) As for the uniform's serving to keep their focus on the game all day, we will be forgiven for wondering if such a focus is consistent with the educational goals of their classroom teachers.

John thought athletes were insensitive and superior. Others I interviewed agreed with this assessment. Should we reconsider of our celebration of athletic success in high schools? We do tend to make heroes of students[14] who are, otherwise, perfectly *ordinary* in the pace of their adolescent development. In fact, the adulation they receive (from the media, parents, administrators, teachers, and many, though certainly not all, classmates) and its inflationary effects on an immature ego, ill prepares them for the exigencies of the real world. If the real world expects more of someone than a high [goals] save percentage, maybe we do them no favors in the long run.

Many artistic students told me that their specialties are undervalued (*"I guess they all really look down on the theatre and the music people just because we're more individualists* [sic] *and they think that's weird"*). They sounded hurt by the neglect, by comparison, of their endeavors, but the fact is no one who talked with me was angry with artists. If, however, the administration were to single out artistic types with permission for special dress, if teachers were to reward them with test postponements, and if newspapers were to review their endeavors with the same excitement that athletics get, we might see a resentment begin to grow towards band and theater participants, that athletes get now.

One of the high schools I visited had a group of senior boys and girls that had a name and identifying clothing. People knew they existed because they would wear t-shirts with the group name on them. These seniors identified themselves with a strong school spirit, going to all athletic events to cheer. Many of them played in sports also. In point of fact they engendered hostility among their classmates (*"These high school cliques are more harsh about who* [sic] *they let in"*). They had a clean-cut, preppy look, but all the students knew they were the biggest "party" crowd. As a social phenomenon they would be the beginnings of a gang presence in the sense that they had unwritten rules about special clothes, membership restricted by invitation, and predictable public customs, including drinking before athletic events and sitting together at school when they ate.

The lunchroom in this school had tables lined up in 30 straight rows of about 25 seats across and most of the students sat according to type: Preps/Socials/Populars at the front, masses of Geeks//Morons/Innocent Stander-Byers in the middle and Goons/Skaters/Bangers at the back, close to the parking lot door. These last rows of tables were referred to as the "drugstore" because of the denizens' reputation for drug use. On the side of the room was an alcove of tables apart from the dining room, as though it had been added after the original construction. One time I indicated that crowded section to a "Social" girl. "Who sits over there?" I asked. She surveyed the faces for several seconds. "Nobody," she concluded. In fact it was the area of tables where the sophomores, newcomers to the school, sat—people who had not yet chosen their look, whose reputations were yet to be made. Taken together: clothes, group name, a sort of "gastronomic geographics"—these things can result in jealousy toward the in-group from the out-group. The crucial difference between this "gang" and a violent one is that there is no fear of physical harm from the in-group. But left unchecked, resentment will erode school spirit every bit as insidiously as intimidation. Since they were all seniors, the group's members were not part of my study. As I interviewed juniors, they were weighing the merits of keeping this unofficial club going next year. We'll call them here, the "Pioneers" and the "Plainswomen."

> Katherine: Um, my boyfriend was a Pioneer. And my sister was a Plainswoman. And a lot of my good friends were Plainswomen. I don't think there's anything wrong with the groups. I guess one thing I wish is that they wouldn't be so clique-y, and that they'd have a sign out in the commissary, "Sign up for Pioneers, sign up for Plainswomen." I wish they'd have that [so] anybody could join in. And that's the way it's supposed to be. But of course it doesn't always end up like that at all. One group takes over. I don't like that. . . . I hate being labeled. I used to be labeled as a Social or a Prep. I hate being labeled. Like at my school, somebody walks through the hall, if you're walking through the commons area, all the front tables are mostly Plainswomen, or all the more In-people. First two tables. And then in the back, there's more of the people who listen to heavier music, dress different, you know, dress more Headbangie type and stuff. And my boyfriend Scott used to hang out with a lot of those people and I used to think oh my god, you know, why am I sitting out here. These are all Druggies. And they aren't. They get labeled that way. Most of em, of all those guys, people I know that sit in the back tables, very few of them do drugs. A lot of the Pioneers do drugs and do all kinds of stuff. But just cause their haircuts are different. And their jeans and their outfits are different. I just really hate labeling people I guess. Usually what happens is that the junior class gets together, if they want to do this. And if they don't, they don't! They'll get together and they'll say hey let's think of a name for us. You know the Pioneers has [sic] always been passed on. But the Plainswomen were something new. Now . . . us juniors, we were gonna start like a group thing. But I said no, I don't want any part in it. Cuz I just knew how it would turn out. Not everybody would be accepted. [They'd say]: "No you guys can't be in it." That's fine. But I don't know if they ended up doing it or not. The Pioneers . . . well one thing, they show great spirit. They always have games. Pioneers are the party throwers. They're the fighters. At sporting events—like at the football games?—they'll start riots! They'll start a big fight with Eastern High. Last year, [at] one of the football games in Eastern, they started a big fight. I really don't think they're all that great. . . . But I mean . . . they're the in thing.

Although students will apply labels to others readily, virtually no one was willing to let a label stick very long to himself (*"My main group of friends [is] all, like, pieces of different groups"*). Students' webs of relationships in this study proved much more complex than labels could begin to describe. "Popular" kids were unliked by the cynical masses. Not-popular kids (un-preppy clothes, unusual haircuts) prided themselves on being democratic in their affiliations (*"Peo-*

ple think I'm a Headbanger because of what I wear but I have friends all over").
John Irving writes, "Everyone of any emotional importance to you is related to
everyone else of any emotional importance to you."[15] But do these "relatives"
all get along? Not socially, not all the time. Several students (all female) whom
we could call group-*neutral* described the difficulty they had navigating the convoluted, multi-cliqued social scene (*"It's hard to have a variety of friends. I'm,
like, working on that right now"*). They felt acutely the opposition to their democratic approach to hanging out, whether they did it for charity or love. For me,
sorting out these groups and their various objectionable attributes engendered a
new respect for anthropologists doing kinship research in a foreign language. If
you thought it was difficult to see why a Trobriand Islander calls his mother's
brother Dad, try pondering the pride of the Prep to call a Headbanger slime:

> Amy: You know, if a guy has long hair and wears like a Metallica shirt, [Preps
> would call them] like, *slime* [or] Headbanger. I'm friends with what—I don't
> want to say Preppie, because I'm friends with [Preppies]—but [I'm friends
> with] what Preppie *people* would consider Headbangers? I'm *friends* with
> those guys! But see, what Headbangers and the "Party-more" types would
> consider Jockey-Socials? I'm friends with those too! Like girls *and* guys! But
> then I have friends from different schools, you know, long-haired guys, stuff
> like that. They like "Metallica," all that kinda stuff? I'm glad though, that I'm
> kinda rounded out in my people that I like.

I asked all students what they thought their friends liked about them as a way
to understand what they themselves looked for in a friend. Most thought that
their friends liked them because they were "fun;" a very close second was that
they could be trusted. (*"My friends and I love to have fun and we count on each
other"*). They explained that a trusted person could keep a secret and never
talked behind a friend's back (*"We tell each other everything and talk about any
problems. You don't have to worry about them going out and blowing it to everyone else. I don't think I could handle that"*). Several implied that exaggeration of
sexual exploits is as much of a problem in the locker room as it ever was. More
than one student said, "I'm mad because so and so said something happened between us that didn't." They were angry, not knowing how to start a rumor to re-
pair their reputation. A rumor will fly around a high school faster than you can
get a hamburger in a drive-through. One way a rumor starts is when a student
discusses something with a person he trusts, only to have it overheard in a public space by others. Two students overhear a personal discussion in the school's
theater. And they are under no oath to keep it to themselves:

> Sharon: [This] was so embarrassing. We were having soccer practice—but it was
> just training, and we didn't feel like running—so we went over by the theater.

And we heard this guy and this girl coming, they're *major* theater people . . . Oh my gosh. [We said to each other] we can't just leave, because they already started talking about someone. They were, like, who they've "done" and stuff like that. And we were, like, we can't just get up and walk out! And we sat in this little corner; we have our legs up like this. And we're, like, Oh my God, [we hope] they can't see us, they can't see us. And then they'd move it, and we'd, like, move over more. We're trying not to laugh. And they were talking about, "Well would you ever fuck this girl, or "Would you ever do this to this girl?" and he goes, "Well, I have," and stuff like that. And we're sitting! And after he said that, we're, like, My gosh, we can't get out now. If they would have walked over a little more, they would have seen us. And we're sitting there with our knees up to our head. I'm like, Oh God, if they ever saw us! And so. Oh my gosh, they were totally . . . and then they started talking about themselves, like, "Well, I don't think I'd ever want to fuck you." It's, God, I don't know, they're two *drama* people. And we're, like, my *gosh*. That was the best. It was so funny. And then we're totally watching because someone was supposed to pick them up or something. We were so embarrassed! We were embarrassed for *them*. And then the next day when we saw them, we were just, like, Oh, my God. Oh, that was the best. We always get into trouble when we're together. . . And we've been going to school together since the third grade.

After the amount of unhappiness students harbored in their hearts for various slights and exclusions, a second reality check for an adult interviewer is the ease with which seventeen-year-old girls (male interviewees never chose to discuss this subject with me) referred to their (or others') sex lives. The topic of sexual activity (for example, choice of birth control or spending the night with someone) came up often enough that it is clear that students are dealing with issues[16] of much more dramatic import (love, lust, obsession, pregnancy, abandonment, despair, revenge) than many adults who know them care to consider. It is little wonder the curriculum looks pale by comparison.

STRESSED

"My hair is out to here (hands over her head). I'm clunching onto everything."

Amber, Grade 11

***

"The body was evolved for adversity."

John Updike[17]

Every day we relate to people in different places who do not know each other, and who only understand us in terms of the one "circle" we occupy with them. Each circle might require a different activity and mode of dress, speech, gaze, facial expression, gesture, posture, movement. Think of the mild social chaos you might cause if you started to show up regularly at the office dressed for softball, or if you acted as though you were by far the youngest person in the room all day long, or sat down to a friend's birthday lunch with the demeanor of someone putting a night crawler on its hook. How would they react if you spoke to your children with the formality you reserve for clergy, or to your colleagues with the impatience you show your children? Learning to keep diverse, non-familial roles and relationships straight is a tall charge. And we assign it first, to five-year-olds. By the time they get to high school, students take for granted that fragmentation is the way of modern life, that one has a core personality but adopts roles in certain situations. Occasionally someone does not keep her roles straight and acts in one situation as though she were in a different one. Adept code switchers themselves, her peers will notice the inappropriateness of her behavior immediately. For example, comporting oneself competitively outside of the academic environment is a school faux pas Bev cannot forgive:

> Bev: This one girl! I was complaining . . . during lunch a long time ago, that I had a lot of homework and I was gonna be really busy tonight and [she] kinda looked at me and says, I'm sorry but you don't know what homework is. And I just kinda looked at her. And I just wanted to say . . . I was so mad! She's in a lot of AP classes and she kinda lets me know it. And that just makes me upset. [I'm] thinking, Why can't you just be yourself instead of being your classes? Just, it's *lunch*, too! Why do you have to act like that anyway? So, that really made me mad.

Students know that successful negotiations in classrooms will vary with the subject, the teacher and the student mix (especially the student leadership) of the class. Their willingness to participate actively in these negotiations—and they are negotiations: for the floor, for the point of view, for the grade—will vary as well, literally from hour to hour, seven times over. The net effect of all this emotional readjusting is stress ("Stress is what changes us"[18]), the third and last "ningee-bingee."

Most of us would think first of tests when we consider the stress of going to school; some of us will have test-taking nightmares years after the grade is recorded. Students report feeling pressured above all to get good grades (44%); getting into college (32%) and fitting in socially (29%) are the two other major teen worries).[19] Tests can give rise to a paranoia ("*sneaky teachers, out to get us*") that resists reasoning. Tests do help everybody keep track of what has been

taught, if not learned, in the curriculum. The word curriculum itself actually derives from the Latin, meaning "the course to be run." Tests are what mark the
road, saying how far they have traveled. Unfortunately, a journey where passing the mileage markers is more celebrated than the scenery is not one you will
return to with pleasure. In high schools, students are accomplishing two trips at
once, their own and that of the curriculum.

Here Eve's personal relationship is the topic of conversation until a test is
announced. She shifts gears deftly:

History Class, February

*There are 19 in this class, 6 boys, and 13 girls. Today I count 9 empty seats in
this bare room; might be due to the exam. The congenial male teacher says to
me, "This is an exam prep period; I'm giving an exam. I warned you about
that! You can come in and see how they prepare for the first 15 minutes." I
take a back seat. There's general commotion in the class as everybody settles
down.*

Eve says something in a low voice to her friend next to her.

Girl (intensely interested): And does he tell you he loves you?

Eve (shrugs): Oh yeah. He's, like, all the time, "Ohhhhh, I loooove you."

*Eve and friend turn back to the front of class to see what the teacher is passing
out.*

Eve (to the teacher): How many pages is this exam?"

*Teacher: You know, Eve, that just kills me. What difference does it make if it's a
thousand questions on one page or five pages with two questions?*

*Eve (turns her palms to the ceiling): Mr. S! I just wanna know. I really get
stressed out!*

*Teacher: Alright, get into your study groups and review this study guide. I want
no cheerleading or yearbook talk or whatever. I don't wanna hear anything
else. I'll cruise the room and you can ask me questions. Get in groups of no
more than two to review, if you want.*

*Tom gets up, takes the paper from the teacher and leaves for the learning dis-
abled classroom. One student braids her hair for the first 10 minutes of class.
An Asian-American girl starts asking two other girls questions from the study
guide. After a moment another girl rushes over from two rows away and says,
"She's not gonna study so I'll be with you (three)." This group now has two
more people than the teacher directed. The teacher ignores it. Two boys sit
side by side and chat, not about the study guide. Tess, a 4.0 student who tells
me history is her "worst, worst, worst" subject, reads all by herself and
doesn't talk to anybody. The teacher finally gives out the exam.*

Girl: There's no choice of all of the above!

*Teacher: If there's no answer calling for all of the above, then you'll have to
make a choice. We talked about that yesterday.*

Commotion as the study groups split up.

Teacher: I don't like book tests. This is the first one I've given this year.

Students: What is this?

Teacher: It's a book test.

Students: Oh, it's from the book.

Teacher: I wrote the last question myself, but if you like this book test maybe we'll do more of them. . . . I don't wanna scare anybody but kids have asked me—I didn't get a chance to correct all these exams—but usually it's the good students who ask, How'd I do, How'd I do? And several came already who took this exam earlier today and said, "How did I do? I thought it was really hard!" Some of them got like 8 wrong who usually get all A's and that'd be, like, a B. So if you finish early, please be polite. Remember: other people are working.

Student (looks over the exam): 8 wrong is a B?!!

Teacher: I don't know what it is; I just used that as an example.

He starts the exam at 1:50, twenty minutes into the class. At 2:04 the first few people are done. They race to the head of the room and pass their paper in and then they go back to their seats and talk to their neighbors so that for the last 20 minutes of class, the handful of people who are still working, hear a lot of conversations. One person hands in her exam, comes back, puts her head down on the desk, sleeps for a little while and then takes out a clothes catalogue and thumbs through it. Tess takes out homework for a different class, ignores the hubbub around her. Tom comes back from the LD room, hands the exam to the teacher. As he passes Eve (whose boyfriend says he loves her) on the way to his back row seat, he crouches a little, puts two fists in front of his face like a boxer, and makes a fast jab with his right, stopping just short of her shoulder. Eve stares straight ahead.

This class period was a slice of high school life. Students talked about different things to each other (*"And does he say he loves you?"*), than to the teacher, (*"How many questions?"*), test anxiety (*"I get really stressed out!"*), cooperative learning (*"Get into groups of no more than two"*), teacher sexism (*"I want to hear no cheerleading talk"*). It had a pull-out remedy for the learning disabled, interest in clothes, interest in appearance and blatant disregard for the teacher's instructions (*"Remember, people are working"*). Most significantly, the teacher talk on this day, as on so many other days, was dedicated to The Test.[20] Teachers seem to operate from the perspective that the testability of knowledge will be in direct relation to its transmittability. This means that evaluation, the worst aspect of schooling, from both sides of the desk, will be neutralized politically. The student will be able to recite the facts, or not. The color of his skin, the forcefulness of his personality or the vividness of his story would play no role in how his answers would be graded. Unfortunately, "testable" also has a direct relationship to "forgettable." Years after the event, students will recite the toppings on a pizza they ate at 2 A.M. while they crammed for a chemistry test, though they could not recognize the symbol for all that sodium. They will recall how the hair stood up on their arms the first time they walked into their big high school, but they could not convert feet to meters without checking first. They will describe the confusion on the face of the teacher (*"a great guy"*) on the light May day, just before class, when they reversed all the furniture in the room. They will recall how he loved it, but not what he taught that afternoon. When Whitehead said that the notion of mere knowledge is a high abstraction, he was promoting a more genuine knowing that included the acute participation of the imagination and all the senses (the taste of the pizza, the feeling of the cool corridor, the sight of a laughing teacher wiping his eyes) in the flow of events, in a given moment, the moment just before it becomes memory. Whitehead[21] warned all of us teachers that the basis of knowing is emotional, but we didn't dare listen.

Teachers test so frequently[22] that a stranger to the site who was unschooled in American public education would think testing was the purpose of their coming together. Although they are two quite different things, the public will commonly equate routine test passing with comprehension of content. The students themselves know better (*"I learned a lot of stuff. I just can't comprehend it all."*) And a secondary school researcher will find as many field notes describing tests as lessons. James Joyce writes, "A good puzzle would be: cross Dublin without passing a pub."[23] My own puzzle would be: cross a school without passing a test. Students themselves are cynical about the usefulness of all this evaluation (*"I don't see how the grade measures how much you've learned, or how much you could learn . . ."*) but they are quite habituated to the routine (*"Every time we read a couple 'a chapters, we have a quiz everyday on it . . . you just know that you have to read it."*) If our major goal in education were to discourage reading for pleasure, testing students every time they read a new chapter would pretty much accomplish it. Continual testing will serve many masters but it will never, in and of itself, make a student want to know more and more.

> Randy: We didn't do any daily work or answer any questions or anything. We just took tests. And that's kinda hard for me because that's where I learn a lot: is when I do my daily work and answer questions? Then I understand things a little better . . . I'm not the greatest at writing essays and I tend to forget things when I'm doing tests. I kinda choke when I take tests. And she has essay tests. And that was really hard for me to get a good grade at all in any of those tests. I don't think I ever got an A on one of those.

Tests will, of course, uncover student slackness and misperceptions (*"I'm going to give you a 5 point quiz. . . . It helps to let me know how you're get-*

ting this.") Tests remind adolescents that the present is related to the future. And tests will compile a record for parents and principals showing that teachers are performing their duties.[24] With all these goals to attain, it is little wonder that tests are the frequent topic of teacher talk. If you ever needed proof that a learner seeks visual verification of the aural message, observe a typical high school classroom for an hour: twenty-five pairs eyes will go up like synchronized garage doors the instant the teacher says, This Will Be On The Test. Teachers know that, when all other seductions have failed, stalking a class with the testing threat will capture students' attention every time. Extrinsic motivation is a drastically different teaching path than intrinsic motivation,[25] as we will see below. In the excerpt that follows, the hardworking Mrs. F tries in vain to corral her wild bunch. The general confusion is complicated by the arrival of two insouciant latecomers. (Alan also figures prominently in the field notes in chapter 2):

English class, March

Kids are really slow in coming in; everybody's talking. It's 2:30, last period of the day. A girl, Jen, comes in completely dressed in green, several slogan pins on her sweater and holding an Irish leprechaun hat that she has filled with candy. She goes down the aisles giving everybody a candy kiss or a butterscotch candy.

When she gets to my place she gives me a candy and I say, "Oh, one for me too?" She says, "Yes."

Boy (to me, about Jen): She's just sucking up.

Alan: B'gosh and b'gorra, it's time for me Irish spring.

Student: Oh, is that ever corny.

Alan (loudly): Will you join me in the shower, Jen?

Jen ignores, or does not hear this. Having given everybody a piece of candy, she sits down. Alan finally sits down.

Teacher: Take a clean piece of paper; put your name in the upper right hand corner.

Students grumble.

Teacher (again): Take a clean piece of paper; put your name in the upper right corner, the upper right hand corner.

Alan: I don't have a pen. Jen, do you have a pen?

Jen: No, I don't.

Alan (calls to another girl by name all the way across the room): Do you have a pen? Do you have an extra pen?

Girl: No.

Alan: (more quietly to Jacy, who's in front of him): Do you have a pen?

Jacy shakes her head without looking back at him.

Alan: Mrs. F, do you happen to have A Writing Utensil?

Teacher: Did you see if anyone else does?

Alan: Not according to them. A pencil. (Then, in a monotone like the history teacher's in Ferris Bueller's Day Off*) Anyone? Anyone? Anyone?*

No one chuckles. Mrs. F gives him one. Next Alan doesn't have any paper. He finally gets a piece of paper from somebody.

On the blackboard the teacher has written, "You are the lost generation."

Teacher: Read this. This is you.

Students (grumbling): Not us. Not us.

Teacher: You are the lost generation, according to Hemmingway. Write what this means.

Alan (loudly): Does that mean I can leave, and say I was lost?

Teacher: No, no. I want you to write down how this applies to work he did in another country.

The kids all look at her blankly.

Boy (abruptly): Okay, pass em forward.

Everybody laughs except Mrs. F.

Teacher (takes a deep breath): It's not any different from anything I did in any other class. They didn't have any of this trouble with it. Explain what the lost generation meant according to work the author did in another country.

The kids are moaning, looking at each other.

Teacher: Think about the story. What it was about, how does it fit? How does it all tie together?

Jen, who had given out the candy, now pulls her Irish hat on. The class laughs, as if they recognize a little act of desperation. Candy time is over.

Teacher: No, no. No hats.

Jen pulls the hat off.

Alan (removing his white painters cap which has the school's team name on the front): Thanks, Jen (sarcastically). Now I have to blind myself.

Alan pulls his hair, which is very long, down in front of his eyes.

After a moment of trying to do this he just puts the cap back on. This is about ten seconds after Mrs. F said, No hats, no hats. She never tells him again to take it off.

Teacher (continues): You can do this, class. You are very bright. They're all looking at her blankly.

Teacher (exasperated): OKAY, LET'S MAKE IT A QUIZ THEN.

The kids grumble.

Teacher: Number one, what city was the hospital in? Number two, what did she sell? Number three, what sport did he play?

Room is soundless. In a flash, the quiz announcement has snuffed out the class personality.

Alan (abruptly): You could give us time to answer.

Teacher (continues): No. 4, okay, narrator. Ben, Larisa, eyes on your own paper, please. What was the reason the narrator was there?

Students: Huh? What?

Teacher: What was the reason the narrator was there, in the story? Number five. . . . Number six, what group of people, according to the author, were very patriotic? Next, who is really into fencing?

Student: His name?

Teacher: No, you don't have to know his name.

Student: What do you want then?

Teacher: What do they call this person? Who was he in the story? Number eight, he tried to speak Italian. What was he not doing correctly? Number nine, why didn't he like marriage? Number ten, how did it end?

Somewhere between question 5 and 6 two students come in. First a girl who goes straight to the last seat in the first row, the seat I had taken originally, until the kid looked at me as if I really should leave it empty. She is wearing black jeans and a black leather jacket zipped right up as if she is outside in the cold. Behind her comes a boy with short red hair. They both slump into their seats and watch people writing.

Teacher (to the girl): Where were you?

Girl: In the office.

Teacher: They didn't give you a slip?

The girl shakes her head.

Teacher: Where were you, Robert?

Robert: Walking around.

The class all laughs.

Teacher (unsmiling): Both of you stay after class.

A girl in the third row asks the late girl what happened.

Latecomer: He said (inaudible). . . . Fuck . . . (inaudible). Then he said I had an angry reaction.

Abruptly, Mrs. F leaves the class. The girl who lived in Europe whom I talk to in gym hasn't written a single word down the whole quiz. The teacher returns after about three minutes with two textbooks that she gives to Robert and the latecomer girl. The late girl goes up and speaks to the teacher then returns to her seat. After a few minutes, the teacher comes down to my desk and says, "Could I ask you to leave? I just can't believe the way they are today." I say, "Oh my God. I'm so sorry. It must be me." She says, "No, no, no. But I'll have to ask you to leave. They're just out of control." I hurry to the door.

Alan: Oh-oh, now you're making me nervous, if the observer has to leave.

Mrs. F slams the gate on their shenanigans by making them write: it will be hard to joke with pals if you have to think of an answer and write it on paper for the adult in control to read. The test is used to recall their attention, remind them of why, really, they are there. We become very aware of the power of the teacher to affect the mood of a group in an instant, and over the long run, the attitude of the group towards the curriculum. Again it occurs to me that if our major goal in education were to discourage writing for pleasure, then using writing as a punishment for academic disengagement will surely get us there.

With all the reminders of the smartest kids' status in school—so that a stranger to any school could discover from students within five minutes who tests out at the top—it is no surprise that students are alert when the topic of testing comes up. High-test performance is rewarded with such intangible things as respect, and tangible things like fast food coupons or even, in this state, lowered car insurance rates. Jake, who works two jobs to pay for his car is conflicted over the cross-currents that the insurance discount stirs up:

Jake: Ah, see I dropped chemistry cuz I was doing really bad and I couldn't really understand it. And I have my own car so I need the B's and the B honor roll to get an insurance break. My insurance isn't too bad right now, but I mean, like I'm gonna buy a new car now too, my car is, like, a piece of crap, to put it bluntly. So. The insurance isn't too bad just with the liability but I wanna get a new car. So. And then I was getting close to 50% in that class and it would have brought my grade point average way down.

Interviewer: I guess I didn't realize that insurance companies look at your grade point when they insure your car.

Jake: Um-hum (yes). Cuz, you get insurance breaks if you get on the B honor roll and you get even bigger insurance breaks if you get on the A honor roll, cuz it just shows what kinda person you are and stuff. Which I don't really think is really good because I'm not really into partying and everything, but I know a lot of people that are on the A honor roll and they just party all the time and they get in car accidents and they still get the insurance break, cuz ah . . .

Interviewer: Cuz they're A students.

Jake: Um-hum (yes). Cuz they copy off of everybody else in their class and on worksheets. On tests, no. I just don't really see a lot of copying on tests. I don't know why—cuz they figure they'll get dropped from the class if they do. But even I copy. I was in German at the time and I copied a girl who was in Germany because she lives on base and I mean, it helps me a lot. See what I do is sometimes I have troubles with it and then I'll just look over and see what she's got and then I'll write down the answer and then I'll try to figure out what goes on.

Interviewer: Okay. Um, to get back to the insurance thing. If you drop chemistry, what does this do to your science requirement to get into college?

Jake: Well, I already have my requireds to get out of high school. Chemistry would help me get into college but it's not essential, especially if I go to the university here cuz they have to accept me.[26]

The relationship of grades to cost of car insurance looms large in the student view. But extrinsic reward systems like this also can have several undesirable results:[27] they actually credit students for less work rather than more, as students opt for a watered-down curriculum to get the easy grade (thereby cheating themselves out of a better education); students are pressured to "help" each other to keep grades up by sharing test answers and homework; students drive more carelessly, knowing that the high grade point mitigates the usual consequences for car accidents; competing with others to get better grades increases stress; the emphasis on competition is at cross purposes with the stated school goal of cooperation; teachers are off the hook to freshen up their teaching and curriculum as students see past their class routine to the reward outside; no one is learning to love math or science or English for its own sake, as a very materialistic motive intrudes itself into what used to be an idealistic enterprise; and finally, bending the rules, or seeing others bend the rules to keep grades up, affirms fully to students that the ends justify the means. Such cynicism among adolescents is one of the more significant and deplorable attributes of their generation. And they acquire it in the competitive atmosphere of school:

CHEATING

"My dad always says, "Think before you do something. Think if I would like it." Well that's not right! Like I'm gonna think of you every time I do something? I mean, think of what you [would] want [me] to do?" (incredulously.)

Angela, Grade 11

***

"Moral education is impossible apart from the habitual vision of greatness."

Alfred North Whitehead[28]

Another cause of the stress that adolescents feel comes from observing, or perpetrating, the widespread dishonesty in the schools. A generation ago, Jules Henry characterized the school's response to cheating as "sloppy" and the adolescent culture in general as having a "slovenly morality."[29] A more recent report shows that 61% of high school students said they had cheated sometime during the past year.[30] Researchers said, "Less than 2 percent of the high school kids . . . get caught. . . . We're creating a society where cheaters do prosper and we can't tell them, honestly, that honesty is the best policy."[31] If cheaters "prosper," it is because their teachers accost relatively few of them. Perhaps teachers are afraid they will not have enough proof to withstand a charge of libel. But neither do all teachers put themselves in a position to obtain proof, by standing sentry-like at the back of the room, or returning early from a school assembly to see who might be rustling around in their desks. Students reported that their teachers did very little to stop cheating, even though, they claimed, teachers know all about it.

Cheating students can resort to many measures: they will try to get the Brain's attention during the quiz, "generously" correct their neighbor's quiz in class (*"You pass it back to the person behind you and when they correct it, they just write in the answer for you."*); find each other in the hallway to get the exam from someone who just took it; steal the lab equipment to replace what they themselves broke; steal the grade book and throw it away; alter the grade book and leave it where they find it (*"In pep rallies you know, everyone will take off and just go back [to the classroom] and change [the grade book] and stuff. And so they'll change their grade and then [those of] their friends. So, you get done with like a lot of [required] work like that!"*), hide the Cliff's Notes or study guides under their exam paper (*"Everyone had Cliff's Notes, cuz they don't read and they cheat on all the quizzes"*); write out the Gettysburg Address the night before on the type of paper they know the teacher will pass out—then pass in the pre-written version; adopt a camouflaging hairdo so they can speak to someone unobserved; pay someone to write an assignment for them; and—in an effort that is certainly as desperate as it must be unsuccessful—write a report on an unread book by copying out the first sentence of every chapter.

Students who object to cheating are not exactly empowered by the system. If they try to blow the whistle they might not be encouraged; and they will never try to stop it again. If a student goes right to the teacher his moral outrage that his lower grade has more integrity than others' perfect score might not be matched by hers (*"She just said, 'Tim, you just worry about your own grade"*).

Deann wishes the chemistry teacher had stepped in earlier. By the time the teacher objects to the cheating, the students have carried on so long that they are put out when he wants them to stop. The net effect is that Deann is more cynical than ever. At seventeen, she now believes that success in Advanced Placement classes is no evidence of excellence, and a B average probably just means that the student is honest.

> Deann: And they're all mad [about getting caught] because they were all cheating before. It was so obvious! And he like finally caught them once so they were pretty mad about that. This group sat in the back, and they all had the same like percentage. They all got As like first two quarters, and now they're all getting Cs. Because he caught them cheating. It's obvious that they cheat and it seems to me that he should do something about it. Part of the problem

is he didn't do something about it until half way through [the term]. If he had just said something the first time! Students from the third period would like write down the questions and the answers for the test and then give them to the 4th period. And so, he switched the test one time and people were just getting them all wrong. I thought that was pretty smart, but it was so far into [the year], that it was going to ruin their grades for like the third and fourth quarter. But, if they'd known at the beginning, then they maybe would have tried harder. There's cheating so bad in that class. And it seems like in some of my classes there is like really bad cheating and then in some there's like barely any at all. . . And it seems to me, a lot of people think that some students who don't get the A's aren't as smart, but it's just they don't cheat as much. There are students who are in a lot of advanced classes who don't know anything, because they've just cheated the whole way through. . . But it's so obvious sometimes. I mean, maybe [the teacher] won't be looking then, but everyone in class knows. I really don't like going to that class because of the people who are in it. I could handle not really liking the teacher—because I don't really like him that much—but I do decent [sic] in the class. And if I don't understand something, I'll go up and ask him. We do things in the lab, and we have to pay for the stuff that is broken and if someone would forget to lock their drawer, people will steal everything out of there. Half of our class is just really bad and then the other half is not that bad. All of us suffer because of half of my class.

How does a cheater rationalize his behavior? Scott is philosophical: Life is hard, risk-taking is fun, seek a balance in life:

Scott: Yeah, but [cheating's] just no big deal. Cuz I mean life's not going to be fair so you've got to take the good with the bad, I guess. That's kind of how I see it. You're not always going to get that break or whatever. And I guess that's kind of what would make me cheat in English. I figure, it's not that I really get angry and stuff. I figure well, if I can get away with, it why not? Cuz no one's ever going to know. It's the easy way out and [studying a given subject] is something I don't want to do already. I have to do it, though. Partly I cheat just to see if I can do it. Cuz it's kind of exciting. It's kind of like doing something for the thrill of it. See if you can get away with it basically.

Others, more altruistic than the self-serving Scott, accomplish a type of charitable work without ever leaving school. As providers of answers (the cheatees), they do good deeds, helping the needy. (The student below, Jim, is the same chronicler of the "rehearsal" of his apology in Chapter 2):

Jim: The girl that sat behind me? And she moved and she was sitting next to me and she moved again, she was in front of me?—was a drug dealer. So this was just great: one time when we had book reports, all the people in my class . . .

asked me to write their book reports for them. In a week. And they'd each give me $5.00. This is when I thought, hey, you know, maybe I can make some money off people's book reports cuz, you know, I read so much. And I'd enjoy that because we could read any book. So this girl in class who had a crush on me asked me. She was the first one who asked me and I was just, like, sure! So. I gave her the "Hunchback of Notre Dame." I [had] read it and I had a typed book report in an hour and a half. And so, I mean, if I've read it before I just skim through it and get the basics and I just write it down and type it. And I guarantee A's. So it was like, OK, for $5.00 you get a guaranteed A, typed paper.

Interviewer: [Would you] Give their money back if they got a B?

Jim: Yup! But everybody got A's. So I mean that was the biggest self-esteem. . . . People still pay me—if you need poems for English class? They give me a couple bucks and I write up a poem.

Interviewer: That's . . . just . . . a riot.

Jim: So, I've been doing book reports and everything since the beginning of my Sophomore year.

Interviewer: Well, you already know you can write for a living.

Jim: Yes. That's what I said. I came home with $40 one day. And my mom's like, Where did you get $40? And I was, like, Well . . . I told her the truth and everything and I said, See, you said I could make money writing and I can! So, I'll be one of those guys in college who does . . . um essays. And, I'm doing senior papers, 500 words for each—500-word biography on Aldous Huxley and then a 500 word essay on Jay Gatsby? I haven't read that book ever so I have to read that. I have to read that book tonight and write a report on it.

Interviewer: You'll love it. What do you get for a 500-word essay?

Jim: Three. Three 500-word essays. 1500 words.

Interviewer: For the same kid? Three essays for one kid? And what do you get for three essays?

Jim: He has to do this to graduate. I gave it to him for $20. Everybody said Oh you should get $50 but I'm, like, you know, he needs it to graduate and you know, he's a hard worker. And this is his third time through. And he works so hard. He just can't . . . he sits there and all these other kids joke, you know, call him names and call him stupid. He really tries though. So, you know.

Interviewer: Is he working, or doing a sport? Or both.

Jim: He's in all the shop classes.

Interviewer: The quality of that [new] writing might surprise the teacher.

Jim: Well, he came up to me after class and he cornered me in the hallway and he said, Don't make it too good cuz she'll know it's not me. And I was just like, All right. Cuz he came up to me today and he said, Jim, you know, you're really smart. You have an A in here, right? I was like, Yeah.

And he's like, So you're really smart, right? And I was like, Well, I guess. And he says, Well, will you do this for me? And I was . . . Ok. So. And other people say, Oh, you're not letting him learn and things like that but . . .

Smart students have always been victimized by classmates who relentlessly seek their help during exams. In fact, one good reason for teachers to put an end to cheating would be to rescue the good students who have stress from the pressure to "share." The academically successful student's moral dilemma is different: not, to-steal-or-not-to-steal, but to be strong enough to ignore the "psssst" in front of a dozen others. Being the smartest kid is already a tough assignment; being smart and aloof would be to condemn yourself to geek hell. Very successful students, especially in math classes, described sharing their homework (*"At lunch, they all go to Eddie, [and say] Let me see your assignment, I know a lot of the people, it seems like they do get pressured a lot into giving out their answers and stuff."*) or their answers during exams. This buys a certain popularity that might be unavailable otherwise. It does seem as though the press to belong, to help each other, to be a pal, often overrides the training in morality that these students bring to school (and conversely the training in morality that they bring to school can be overridden precisely because alienated kids feel no sense of belonging there). It is as though the student subculture has a code of its own that is written over the school door, visible only to those below a certain age: "Enter here and we might let you become one of us—a more important aspect of your education than anything else."

NOTES

1. Tan, Amy (1995), *The Hundred Secret Senses*, NY: G.P. Putnam's Sons, p.43.
2. 68% of students feel that violence in their schools is just a small problem or not a problem at all: The Shell Poll (1999).
3. Lee, Harper (1960), *To Kill a Mockingbird*, NY: Warner Books, p. 33.
4. McGuffey, William Holmes (1879), *McGuffey's First Eclectic Reader*, NY: Van Antwerp, Bragg & Co.
5. In 1990, the average American child age 2 to 5 years watched over 27 hours of television per week. See: Centerwell, Brandon S. (1992), "Television and Violence: The Scale of the Problem and Where To Go From Here," in *The Journal of the American Medical Association, 267, n22*, p.3059 (5).
6. Goodlad, John (1984), *A Place Called School*, NY: McGraw Hill, p.97.
7. *The Far Side*® by Gary Larson© 1983 by FarWorks, Inc., All Rights Reserved. Used with permission.
8. Ackerman, Diane (1990), *A Natural History of the Senses*, NY: Random House, p.305.
9. Whitehead, Alfred North (1948/1974), *Science and Philosophy*, NY: Philosophical Library, p. 37.
10. In North Dakota there are 642,200 people, with the following ethnic distribution: 92% white, 4.9% Native Americans, 1.2% Latino, 0.6% African Americans,

0.6% Asian, 0.4% who identify themselves as "other" and 1.2% who report 2 or more races. (2000 U.S. Census).

11. Eckert, Penelope (1989), *Jocks and Burnouts: Social Categories and Identities in the High School*, NY: Teachers College Press.

12. Concern over school violence continues even though school murders nationally dropped from a peak of 52 in 1991 to 13 in 1999 (Associated Press: Sept. 7, 2000: "FBI Urges Officials' Attention to Violence-Preoccupied Students").

13. Students' wearing uniforms in public schools are said to correlate with: ". . . decreasing violence and theft, preventing gang colors and insignia, instilling discipline, resisting peer pressure, increasing concentration on school, and recognizing intruders who come into the school." U.S. Dept of Education. *Manual on School Uniforms*, February, 1996, op cit: Noll, J.W., ed. (1999), *Taking Sides: Clashing Views on Controversial Educational Issues* (10th edition), pp.311–312.

14. Eckert, Penelope (1989), *Jocks and Burnouts: Social Categories and Identities in High School*, NY: Teachers College Press.

15. Irving, John (1996), *Trying to Save Piggy Sneed*, NY: Arcade Publishing, p.372.

16. 58.9% of 17 year olds in North Dakota reported having sexual intercourse. See: Wessman-Downey, V. and R.G. Landry, "Self-Reported Sexual Behaviors of High School Juniors and Seniors in North Dakota," *Psychological Reports, 80*, 1357–1358, 1997.

17. Updike, John (1981), *Rabbit is Rich*, NY: Alfred A. Knopf, p.400.

18. Gilbert, Robert N., and Robins, Mike (1999), *Welcome to Our World: Realities of High School Students*, Thousand Oaks: Corwin Press.

19. The Shell Poll (1999).

20. Every published standardized test in America is owned by a company which also publishes textbooks, giving rise to the question of the relationship of testing to the creation of markets for books. See Daniels, H. (1995): "Whole Language: What's the Fuss?," in Levine, D., R. Low, B. Peterson, and R. Fenario, eds., (1995), *Rethinking Schools: An Agenda for Change*, Scranton, PA: W.W. Norton.

21. "Ninety per cent of our lives . . . are governed by emotion. Our brains merely register and act upon what is telegraphed to them by our bodily experience. Intellect is to emotion as our clothes are to our bodies: we could not very well have civilized life without clothes, but we would be in a poor way if we had only clothes without bodies," in: Price, Lucien (1954), *Dialogues of Alfred North Whitehead, As Recorded by Lucien Price*, Boston: Little, Brown and Company, p. 231.

22. "Tests took up a collective quantity of 20 million school days in 1990 at a cost of $800 million," in Supoviitz, J. A. and R.T. Brennan (1997), "Mirror, Mirror on the Wall, Which is the Fairest Test of All?: An Examination of the Equity of Portfolio Assessment Relative to Standardized Tests," *The Harvard Educational Review (67)*, pp. 472–498.

23. Joyce, James (1961), *Ulysses*, NY: Random House, p.4.

24. "Tests that measure as little and as poorly as multiple-choice tests cannot provide genuine accountability. Pressure to teach to the test distorts and narrows education. Instead of being accountable to parents, community, teachers and students, schools become

"accountable" to a completely unregulated testing industry," in: *Fair Test*, The National Center for Fair and Open Testing, Cambridge, MA, www.fairtest.org.

25. See: Ryan R.M. and E.L. Deci (2000), "Self-determination Theory and the Facilitation of Intrinsic Motivation, Social Development and Well-Being," *American Psychologist, 55*, (1), pp. 68–78.

26. Four year colleges in North Dakota require the student to graduate from a high school that has a certain core curriculum, have an overall GPA of 2.25 and an ACT score above 17.

27. The use of extrinsic rewards results in a decrease in interest in the activity itself. See Deci, E.L. and R.M. Ryan (1985), *Intrinsic Motivation and Self-Determination in Human Behavior*, NY: Plenum; and Kohn, A. (1993), *Punished by Rewards: The Trouble with Gold Stars, Incentive Plans, A's, Praise, and Other Bribes*, Boston: Houghton Mifflin. Others suggest that the use of standardized tests results in an increase of feelings of hopelessness and decreased intrinsic motivation. See Caine, G., and R.N. Caine (1999), "Bringing the Brain Into Assessment," *The High School Magazine*, March.

28. Whitehead, Alfred North (1929/1967), *Aims of Education and Other Essays*, NY: Macmillan, p.69.

29. Henry, Jules (1963), *Culture Against Man*, NY: Vintage, p.280.

30. Josephson, Joseph and Edna Josephson (1998), "Report Card on the Ethics of American Youth," Marina del Ray: Josephson Institute of Ethics.

31. ibid.

Chapter Four

Bewildered

"... And algebra, I just don't get."

Liz, Grade 11

***

"Meaningful knowledge must be constructed under vital conditions of experience which require us to . . . hunt for connections."

John Dewey[1]

Students leave elementary school having had the advantage of one teacher all day, all year. Even if they were not good friends, elementary teacher and student usually had achieved a certain resigned understanding between themselves. This teacher could predict the student's responses to topics, teams, competition; she knew his tastes in reading, food, music; she understood his allergies, enemies, habits and hobbies; she knew where to situate him, and where he situated himself, within the class. An elementary teacher is apt to say, "I'm a little worried about Kate; I've noticed she's really quiet this week." The high school is a different place: the quieter Kate is, the *less* the teacher will notice her. An overbooked high school teacher doesn't worry about quiet students; he thanks God for them. Keeping track of 125 names in his grade book, various preparations for five uneven classes, and of his own progress getting through a staggering amount of disparate material, leaves a teacher precious little time for deep reflection on all those disparate personalities—let alone which mode of instruction suits which one best. The high profile students, successful or failing, warrant the teacher's attention. This helps explain why a parent might leave the first teacher conference in the fall with the funny feeling the teacher did not seem to connect his shy son's name with a face. The teacher reported a grade, but relayed no personal anecdote or individual insight.

Many unhappy memories of junior high come from the experience of being taught for the first time by a turn-taking crew of six strangers ("*[in elementary school] a teacher used to explain it. Now they're just figuring you know how to do it. And I don't know how*"). By the time they get to high school students know that feeling separated or unrecognized will describe a hefty portion of their daily experience. When I asked eleventh graders what kids who were coming to high school for the first time did not yet know, they said, "This is a huge place. This is a different place. You will have more freedom here, but you will be lonely here." Once I told a colleague that I was researching how it feels to be a junior in high school and she said, "Be sure you say what it's like to get lost in the shuffle when you're just average. Be sure you say high school is a great place for the "stars" and the learning disabled, but that the run-of-the-mill kid slips right through the cracks." Frustrated, this highly educated professional moved her family out into the country, where teachers would recognize her children in the fullest context of small town life, and where they would have a better chance for the experiences that would earn them their self-esteem.

If they are able to empathize with the plight of the tired, overbooked teacher, some students might recognize their own role in reversing the situation. Here Jackie describes how she always goes the extra mile to ensure her own progress. Once again the interpersonal relationship between student and teacher is seen by the student as the sine qua non of academic success:

Jackie: Some [teachers] care. Some of them. But a lot of them just don't want to have the problems; don't want to deal with it. [They seem to say] It's your life, you know . . . I know a lot of them wouldn't understand. A lot of them are just like, "Well, you're in my class now. You have to do *this*." Most of them aren't like that. But there are still some like that . . . that's how Miss D [is]: There's no connection between her and the students . . . you don't feel like she'd care if you had a problem. So you don't communicate with them . . . I think you have to have an understanding between student and teacher . . . But, there's so many kids and one teacher. *You* have to make the effort to knowing [sic] the teacher . . . be more outgoing, ask questions, talk more, get to know what they think. . . . That's where you begin in school . . . If I had a problem I'd go to the teacher say look, this is what my problem is, this is how it's gonna be and I can't do what you want me to do right now. And a lot of them would understand. But you have to go to them. If you don't get your assignment *they*'re not going to come to you [saying], Well, how come? They're going to say, "You didn't do it; obviously you didn't want to." I have to get in touch [with teachers]. Like next year is going to be pretty easy cause I know some of my teachers. Cuz I've already had em? Cuz your first year at Jefferson, you don't know anybody, anything and you're just like, o*KAY*. And you have to get to know your teachers or else . . . I don't know (sighs).

It sounds as though you have to get to know your teachers or you will never be able to hand something in late (*"I can't do what you want me to do right now"*).

I think given how much evaluation goes on in a typical day, and given how uncorrelated the curriculum is (so no teacher ever knows what another is requiring unless by happenstance) it is inevitable that the rapidly running waters of testing and agitation of personal problems will cause a whirlpool of anxiety more than once in a grading period. Jackie's advice is: Get to know your teacher so if you have a problem, you can go to them. I translate that this way: Get to know your teachers so they will believe you when you describe a conflict between their test and your life.

A successful class is a conversation involving an older voice and younger voices, both parties to the lesson. In their training classes, prospective sales people learn that "telling is not selling." The customer should be engaged, made to inquire, an active conversant in the very sales-pitch aimed *at* her. Although it is a crass comparison, secondary pre-service teachers would do well to consider the same advice about engaging the listener. They will say that they are going to be teachers of biology or history or music, forgetting that they are going to be teachers, first, of adolescents. Perhaps the prospect of facing so many unknown personalities is daunting, or maybe the school structure—which they know well by experience—constrains freewheeling creativity. Most probably the notion that the teacher can reveal himself to be less of a final authority (*"[if they would] just be human!"*) and still secure respect, is very foreign to them. Whatever the case, many teachers resort to the mode of teaching they observed in college: impersonal information delivery (*"Teachers have a kind of formality: they don't seem to care if you learn"*). By honoring the material before the students, the teachers make students feel unseen: "she seems to be teaching herself instead of to us;" "he gets going on his own little stories," or "off on his own thing."[2]

We know that the more people involved in a social or political situation, the more diluted is each person's sense of responsibility for what happens there. So for example, the more witnesses to an accident, the longer the response time before someone seeks help. Once students hit high school they are sadly aware that the response time to their personal or academic accidents is slower than it used to be, as the watchdog responsibility for their progress is spread over six teachers or more. Some might say that this is appropriate, given the fact that in real life, especially in a competitive arena like college, the individual will have to make his own solitary way. Maybe high school is where you should get used to this idea, nice and early. Coddling time is over. High school is a boot camp for the big, bad, impersonal world. Such a utilitarian rationale implies that there is no necessary relationship between a sense of belonging and meaningful work; that you don't need the first to have the second. Such a rationale implies that there is no necessary relationship between meaningfulness and genuine learning. But students in this study would tell you urgently, that such a rationale is completely wrong.

NEGLECTED

"There are very few teachers who actually, you know, cared if you learned."

Ken, Grade 11

***

"The underlying assumption of a person in any mass society is that most people are indifferent to him or dislike him or that only a tiny minority like him. Under such circumstances it is hard to imagine what could poison social relations more than withholding signals of affection and approval."

Jules Henry[3]

Perhaps it is not so much that teachers are indifferent to students so much as it is that they believe their first obligation is to their course content. In the line-up for teacher devotion, students simply have to yield to the lesson. With so much to cover, there's little time for a teacher to send "signals of affection." Is that really their job? Aren't there enough signals of affection going around their rooms as it is? And if social relations are poisoned, well this is not a bowling league; we're educating future college students here! Students needing approval just have to do well. Show up, step up, get the job done. It's not very complicated: the approval follows naturally, in the form of a grade. Yet curriculum-centeredness, as opposed to child-centeredness, feels like a form of neglect to students (*"Teachers don't care a thing about how much homework they'll give you"*) and they resent it.[4]

Maryanne: Oh gosh, I took the advanced chemistry, "Chemstudy," this year? And we all went in there knowing that it was gonna be really hard. And that's another case of . . . at first I really didn't like the teacher. It was like history where he'd write all the notes on the board and you'd copy it down. And [he] gives your assignment. And it was really hard. And for a while, we adjusted to that. We were doing okay, and then, you know, we start building [knowledge]. It's another "building" thing? And we didn't really understand it as well as we should have and it got really kind of bad there for a while. I was lost. I mean . . . with golf season and things? If you're gone for one day, you know. And he's one of these people that's really antsy and fidgety and kind of

stubborn? And you ask him a question and he [says] Well, it's right there! It's
on the board! What else is there? And if you ask a question he takes it offensively, like you're discrediting him or something. [As if you were saying] Oh
you didn't teach this right. . . . One thing he won't do is, he won't stay past
3:30. So, like, we're doing "qual tests" and that's where, in the lab, you're trying to tell what the chemical is? And if [you've been] gone—if you don't have
a free period—you're kind of out of luck. Cause he won't stay. So you have
to get out of another class, which [makes] that [other] teacher . . . mad and
then it kind of creates problems. But with me it wasn't a problem because I
had a free hour.

Interviewer: Yeah. But, he's not required to stay after 3:30?

Maryanne: I guess not. I assume teachers probably aren't. But most teachers are
willing to stay a few minutes anyway.

Maybe Maryanne misconstrues her teacher as "defensive" to her questions.
But she has reason to feel neglected when he will not stay in school beyond
the last bell: he is not merely impatient with the person who needs clarification (or is he impatient with her preference for the golf team that pulls her out
of class at crucial times?), he is too impatient to stay "late." And "late" is the
one time of day when the confused student might have the guts to reveal her
ignorance; all those other non-golfing science wizzes have gone home. Com-
pounding this for Maryanne is the fact that his refusal to stay might cause her
to incur the wrath of another teacher. So the chemistry teacher is double
wrongdoer: he neglects his students and makes trouble for them with another
teacher. Knowing how little the typical student cares about school subjects,
and how much she cares about teachers' views of her, this latter consequence
is the one that is really bothersome.

We saw in Chapter 2 that students credited or blamed teachers for their successes or failures. Given the emotional investment students make in the ped-
agogic relationship it was understandable that many sounded bewildered by
teachers whom they perceive to be unwilling to work at involving the class or
making themselves clear. For me students' plaintive descriptions of feeling
neglected or mystified were a low point in our conversations because I believe teachers do care a lot about their students. Does anyone enter this profession for its remarkable remuneration? Don't teachers do this job expressly
because they enjoy kids? Isn't being with adolescents—that quirky, funny,
sensitive age—the real joy of teaching? Apparently not for all teachers. The
sense that their presence is unimportant to their teachers,[5] or that their comprehension of the material is of no consequence is felt by many.[6] The truth is
that feeling unseen or confused makes profound commitment to the work that
teachers assign virtually impossible. Apparently you have to do it for yourself. Those of us who have spent time in public schools know that such a

student—the one who, we might say, already belongs to her future—the student who is a self-starter (in Spanish, the "chispa," or spark) is not characteristic of the masses. Powerfully self-motivated students have their eye on a goal beyond high school, usually a prestigious college or a competitive career. And their ambition is a bonus for a teacher because in their quest to succeed they often serve as teachers themselves, of their teachers. But the average student cannot or will not study so hard she has new knowledge to share in class. And furthermore, sharing what you learned over and above the required work is a classic example of a teacher's pet. So there's not a multitude of ambitious students, and without them, a teacher concentrates more on the material, than on getting it across. And manages in the meantime to get a reputation of bewildering students instead of teaching them.

Occasionally, even in the presence of a multitude of ambitious kids, as in the Advanced Placement class described below, a grim teacher can make students feel neglected. Some of these students thought the teacher was sneaky, but it actually was an old fashioned case of personal class dislike:

Patty: The only thing that saves most of the people, if they like history is if they just want to read it on their own. Or, you know, they have a good background and they know [the topic]. And it's just really hard. I don't think he does any preparation for the class. He asks, Did it mention this in your book? I don't think he reads the book! And that bothers me too, cuz when we get a worksheet, it's like 5 words. And it says, Define. And when we get a test we get a blank sheet and he says, Write 40 things that you know about the chapter. And he just doesn't put any effort into the class at all, I don't think. . . . Usually he'll throw us into groups. And hand us a worksheet and say identify these things. And then we'll never talk about those things again. Or sometimes he'll get up there and he'll start lecturing and things, and then he'll say, Well did it mention this in the book? And we're like well, I don't know. He says, Well look it up. I'm not gonna tell you if you don't know. He won't answer questions. He will not answer any questions and if you don't know something he never goes through it. He says it's not his responsibility; it's ours. Well, does anyone else know? You know, we have a few people that are in there and they're talkers and they can talk circles and never say anything. And that really frustrates him. And then he just totally shuts down says, Well, look it up. Figure it out. I'm not gonna waste time if you didn't read. That's his favorite thing: "I'm not gonna waste time if you didn't read." And I mean, 40-page chapters is [sic] a lot to read in one night! You're not gonna absorb it all . . . But any assignment we do, we don't get credit for. . . . It's just for the sake of doing it. He just says read the chapter and then we have a test on it. And they're hard tests and we don't really discuss it in class. It's really a college course, I guess, but there's just something about it that doesn't work. It's busy work. He'll give us a worksheet and never look at it again. We'll spend 2 hours doing it and he won't even ask to see it. And you know, we have all the really smart people. And he'll give us worksheets and he'll say, "Oh look over this for tomorrow." And then he'll say, "Well hand it in today, done. And then he'll take a 50 point grade on it . . . it's kind of like he's out to get us? It's kind of sneaky the way he does things. I just don't like it.

Although I never observed the AP class referred to above, I was a regular, early morning visitor to another history class this same teacher taught. There he was funny and energetic, right on top of things. Any observer would say he worked hard to keep everybody focused in class, that he seemed fascinated by the study of history. One day as we walked down the hall together we talked generally about the contrast between teaching the two types of classes, advanced and regular. That is when I learned how much he resented the AP class for its "smart alecks," who "talk too much," think "they know everything," and whose "parents think nothing of taking them out of school for a ski trip." He wasn't exactly "out to get" this class, but he surely was resentful of what he perceived as their superior attitude and social status. And the students felt his resentment loud and clear.

A teacher who will not talk at a crucial point in the curriculum, the tried and true "teachable moment, " loses a good opportunity to make the obscure clear, or to synthesize conflicting views (*"In English where I've not had the same answer [as the teacher] . . . when I try to discuss it—I am ignored"*). The students' questions, like their obsessions, can evaporate overnight. Here a tired teacher who might have sat through this old film three or four times a year for thirty years goes away without noticing students need him for clarification. Will they remember their question in the morning?

History Class, March

About quarter of nine Becky comes flying in from the parking lot and we talk for a while in the cafeteria before her first class. She seems to be in a bad mood. She describes an argument with her best friend, Karen last night. Karen keeps asking to borrow Becky's car, which is strictly against the rules of Becky's parents. Then she tells me that yesterday in History they had a substitute teacher.

Becky: She was as dumb as snot. Randall hid the remote and she didn't even know that they had a remote, so the VCR stopped and the substitute keeps going, What's wrong with this, what's wrong with this? We were all dying laughing. She had two teachers in there trying to figure out what was wrong with the television.

The bell rings so Becky and I rush off to History. When we come into the class, Randall, who had hidden the remote on the substitute teacher yesterday, is talking to the real teacher, now returned:

Randall (at the top of his voice): Something was wrong with the television yesterday. It kept skipping.

Teacher (looks really worried): The tape was bad? The tape was that bad?

Randall: No! The tape is Very Fine! But Something was wrong.

Teacher (looks thoroughly confused): I don't understand it, I don't understand it.

People around Randall are trying to stifle their snickers at all of this.

Teacher: Okay, I have a note from the Substitute that you were not watching the film yesterday so be on notice: I WILL GIVE A TEST ON THIS MOVIE AND IT WILL COUNT AS A REGULAR TEST, SO TAKE NOTES.

The teacher turns on the machine. The videotape of The Grapes of Wrath *is working perfectly today.*

Teacher: This shows the utter poverty and hopelessness of the people. They had picked up and moved from Oklahoma.

Class is silent.

Randall: When was this film made?

Teacher: 1948.

Randall (getting his revenge on the snitch-substitute): The Substitute said it was 1938.

Teacher makes no reply. The movie begins; lights off. The teacher retires to the back of the classroom where he sits at a student desk, doesn't watch the movie. He seems to be dozing or maybe reading something on his lap, it's hard to tell in the dark. Becky's doing homework with a book open. I count 8 kids doing work with pens in their hands, textbooks open. One boy is right next to the teacher, not watching the film, working away on something else. One girl right in front of him is writing rapidly. I don't know how they can see in the dark. Becky and Randall confer on her homework. Then she reads a note passed to her from the estranged Karen.

Finally after 45 straight minutes of the movie, with two minutes left to go to the bell, he turns off the video; the movie will have to be continued tomorrow. The teacher says absolutely nothing to the students and walks out of the room. People gather up their books. Bell hasn't rung yet.

Boy (to no one in particular): I don't know why these people didn't eat vegetables since they were starving in the film.

Girl 1: They didn't have any

Boy: Of course they did. They were in California.

Girl 1 (indicating departing teacher's back): Ask him. They didn't!

Girl 2: I can't figure out who's who. I just can't keep the people in this movie straight.

Girl 3: I was asleep the whole time.

Karen (turns around to them): We saw this movie in English.

Boys and girls together (incredulously): You saw it already?

Karen: Yeah.

Girl 2: I wish I had seen the beginning yesterday.

Girl 3: Nobody saw anything yesterday.
The bell rings and everybody bolts out.

The substitute teacher's arrival presents the golden opportunity for class clowns and malcontents. So Randall's excellent adventure with the remote control is just slightly better than run-of-the-mill harassment of The Sub. What I find interesting is that when the teacher discovers that the class "had not been paying attention" he immediately threatens a test on the material. Not, Well maybe the substitute didn't know how to catch their interest in this film, so I'll do it now; but, Take this down for future reference or you'll be SORRY! The students don't take the test threat seriously because it is used so frequently. As an incentive, it is spent. They'll worry about it the day before the test (and then they'll whine for a review). And anyway, it'll never happen. Furthermore, there's something counterintuitive about the teacher's tactic: threats are useful for getting people to avoid doing things (jail time for crime, detention for tardiness, F's for failure). Promises of rewards are useful for getting people to *do* things (release time for professional development, early dismissal for travel to the big game, A's for achievement). We note that the teacher is saying implicitly, You will be *rewarded* with an A if you pay attention to the movie. But it's implied crankily. He's unhappy with them; they embarrassed him to the substitute. She probably thinks he lets this class go nuts all the time.

In the defense of the teacher, making this tough class see the "reward" of gaining new insights, having an aesthetic experience, or integrating knowledge from many sources—all by paying attention to *The Grapes of Wrath*—is a tough challenge. Obviously just predicting such outcomes to them will not ignite enthusiasm. Teenagers for the most part are distracted by interests in, and affections for quite different things. What would ignite enthusiasm is the teacher's own energy. My mother used to warn us, "There's nothing catchier than nerves," as she tried to get her five children to relax about some upcoming thing. One child suffering the pangs of anxiety was plenty; five would constitute group therapy. Maybe I am making essentially the same point, but I think there's nothing catchier than excitement.[7] If the teacher were really happy to see this film, and conveyed a genuinely spirited anticipation of it, the students would respond. They don't really want to be bored. Watching his enthusiasm they might get curious; they might want to "have whatever he's having." Instead, these students scoop up the hour to do other homework. And why not? The teacher himself nods right off as soon as the lights go down.

Students are well aware there is a lot of material to learn: they are the ones who lug those thick textbooks from locker to home and back again. The more circumspect among them manage to give their busy teachers the benefit of the doubt ("*I guess they try to get everything they can [in], that is supposed to be done within that year*") or to sympathize ("*If I had to teach people, I'd be bitter too*"). But since they spend so much time thinking of how to please their teachers, students would appreciate it if their teachers spent a little time returning the favor.

> Erica: But my teacher kinda ruined it for everyone, you know? He was a computer teacher. We'd go in there one day and he'd write the notes on the board? He wouldn't explain 'em to us at all. We would just write them down. We'd be done, that would take the rest of the class. We'd go in there the next day and he'd say [Make this period a] study hall. We wouldn't do anything. And then, you know, next day he'd have a movie for us? On something [we're] not even [studying], like, it would be on space or something. The next day he'd give us a review sheet and the next day we'd have a study hall again. He wouldn't talk to us at all. It was like he was scared of us or something. And then the next Monday, we'd have another stupid movie and then we'd have the test the next day. Nobody knew what was going on. After a while you know, we figured out just study your notes in the study halls and you'll do OK but . . . that was bad. They got mad at him for doing that.
> Interviewer: Who? The administration?
> Erica: Yeah.

NEGLECTED GIRLS

"Mr. W is such a pervert: he said any girl who wore a bikini to swimming would get an A."

Maureen, Grade 11

***

"No one can expect, of course, to go through life without meeting discouragement and criticism, but every failure is more costly if it is accompanied by the implied message from outside, and the hidden belief within, that little more could have been expected."

Mary Catherine Bateson[8]

I noticed very early in my year of observations the relative absence of girls' voices in classrooms. I hoped that students I interviewed would mention their reactions to this state of affairs. When they did not, I decided to ask every student an intentionally provocative (and poorly-constructed) question: True or False: boys talk more in class because they are smarter. I got two very consistent replies. All replied that boys are not smarter. Why then did they speak out more often? Aside from a handful who said, Oh I have a class where the girls do all the talking, most agreed that boys indeed participated more. But they explained it differently, according to gender—and in terms of the other gender's shortcomings. Boys said that girls talked less in class because they were shy, distracted, disinterested, afraid to look dumb. They explained to me that girls were airheads. Boys summed up matter-of-factly, Boys Are Naturally Aggressive. Girls said boys talked more in class because they were loud, obnoxious, craved attention, created more heat than light. They explained to me that boys were show-offs. Girls summed up matter-of-factly, Boys Are Naturally Aggressive. With this genetic prediction across both genders it would be a strong girl indeed who would violate it. A strong girl with a helpful teacher.

Virtually every adolescent I talked with claimed that girls did not enjoy competitive conversations in the classroom ("*I don't know if it's just in their nature, but girls just can't fight back, unless they're Italian or something*"). To be aggressive in a discussion you need a momentary suspension of genteel concern for the other's feelings, and perhaps some girls felt they had less of the wherewithal for such suspension. Obviously we should hesitate to say categorically that all of one sex are "naturally" more this or that. But I do have a question, based, as Whitehead once said, on no confusing research: Could it be that boys are habituated earlier than girls to risk themselves in competition? The type of play boys typically engage in Western societies, on summer sandlots or winter rinks, has a sort of rhythm: swinging/missing, aiming/missing, trying/finally, succeeding.[9] Could this be a friendly training-in-public-failure? Updike said the world runs on push. Maybe it's boys who learn this attitude as youngsters.[10] (Others say that girls learn that the world runs on care.[11]) It could be that what boys learn earlier than girls is that—luck and sheer endowed talent aside—success actually requires steely indifference to how others will regard their first failed attempts. Young Deweyans all, they believe experience is the best teacher. They have to try again. The game goes on. The team will not wait. Later, to the relief of their answer-seeking teachers (and the consternation of the women they marry) many boys will seem somewhat less concerned about the social consequences of imperfection.

Louise: Maybe um, I think maybe cuz guys aren't scared of getting embarrassed if they ask something whereas girls think, well somebody will laugh at me if I say that or you know, if I ask that question well are they gonna think I'm dumb . . . I think maybe girls are more self conscious about that. [In German class] maybe the whole first half of the year where I'd like be saying hardly anything because I was so scared that even if I did, that my answer would be wrong. Cuz there's some teachers that, if your answer's wrong, they'll drill on you. So [I'm] just kinda are scared to answer sometimes. In German I was just scared of admitting to being lost. [Teachers will say] weren't you listening the ten times I said it before?

Girls were more likely to compare themselves unfavorably to the other sex (*"I think guys are smarter. Or maybe I'm just stupid"*). And some just assumed that their teachers shared this negative comparison (*"[If I ask a question a teacher would act like] 'Oh you're blond, you're dizzy—of course you don't understand that"*). As a female with a long tenure in the student role (and the mother of a daughter) I found the extent to which girls actually anticipated a dummied-down role for themselves[12] in class frustrating (*"Everybody knows I'm not that bright of a person. I made the B honor roll though"*). Invariably girls, not boys, apologized to me for claiming to be good in a subject, as if, with convoluted reasoning, the mention of success would have me think less of them.

The dominance of boys' voices in classrooms is documented well and demonstrated daily. Teachers claim they do not favor one gender over another, but the numbers don't lie.[13] The large majority (65%) of teachers of required subjects in the schools I researched was male. The frequent high ratio of male teacher to male students may well have contributed to the comfort level of male students to engage in conversation—and to the discomfort level of the female students[14] (*"[Girls] are just more timid because a lot of the teachers are very intimidating. Mr. D could tear any girl to shreds and not even think about it"*).

> Kay: My chemistry . . . is college prep chemistry. Um, the teacher doesn't think that girls should be in enriched classes. He doesn't believe that girls can do that kinda stuff? At least . . . all the girls in my class have come to that conclusion. . . . He gave out science awards. All three of them went to guys! No girls. You know, if girls ask a question, [he'll say] Well it's right there. Look at it. And the guys ask a question he'll go for 35 minutes on explaining this question that takes a yes or no answer. There's just teachers [who believe] . . . girls shouldn't be in this class so therefore I'm not gonna pay attention to them and they'll go away.

Even natural allies like female teachers can favor the boys' presence in class (*"She's a really good teacher, but she likes boys more than girls. I've talked to counselors, and they say, Yeah, Mrs. R. is like that: she likes boys more than girls"*). And some school counselors, whom we would presume to be sensitized by their training, prejudge their female students:[15]

> Bev: Well my shop teacher in 9th grade was [sexist] until he realized that I had more brainpower than half the guys in that room. I mean most of 'em [have

to be told] Pick up your pencil; write your name on a piece of paper. They had to sit there for about 5 minutes and think about it before they could do it because they were so out of it. Half my classes next year are gonna be Advanced Placement. And . . . my counselor said, Well are you sure you're gonna be able to handle all this? And I'm like . . . I can *handle* it. Trust me. I know what kinda class loads I can handle. He's thinking that I'm gonna be too busy with guys. Yeah, guys are part of my life but they're on the back burner compared to my education.

At one time, the presence of girls in Industrial Technology class was unusual. Liz is thrilled to have a drafting class she can take in which she can succeed—not fail chronically as she has math. She found geometry easy but told me, "I don't do good in your algebras." This class had many academically unsuccessful boys but it is Liz who has to fight to hold her own as the boys frequently make fun of her. Even the teacher, who is fond of Liz and has been very patient as she struggled through some very difficult emotional times, cannot resist the urge to join in. Why, we wonder, if Liz is one among the many "Metalheads" who find success in the drafting class, is she the only one who gets ridiculed?

Drafting class, January

There are 20 drafting tables facing one direction and 20 classroom desks facing the other direction. It's a very big room. There are also 12 computers in here. There's a real hubbub in the class. The teacher raises his voice to be heard. Everybody drifts in with pop cans. The rule about no pop cans has been forgotten in the two weeks since Mr. P announced it. Several students who look non-traditional mention that they really enjoy this class because the teacher is so "laid back." One kid walks in one minute past 8. The teacher raises his eyebrows as if to say, What's your excuse? He's very strict about tardiness but he doesn't care about the pop drinking. The kids open the top drawer of their drafting desk and rest the can in there upright or if it's a plastic bottle, they take a swig, put the cap back on, lay it down on its side in the bottom drawer and close it. The sound of metal drawers banging closed is constant.

Teacher: Okay come up and take the quiz on chapter 16, go back to your seats and do it. Then when you're finished come up and get the quiz on the next chapter.

The quiz is on elevations. The boy in the last row last seat who had come in with me from the outside without a jacket on this freezing cold day is reading a Seventeen *magazine. He's ignoring the instructions to come up and get his quiz. Liz comes to the back of the room from the second row and looks at the magazine with him and they're talking about what they're looking at. After a while the teacher reminds him, "Are you gonna take the quiz?" Student says, "Yeah."*

Teacher: Liz, come back up here.
Liz: Yeah.

She ignores him for a few seconds, looks at the magazine, says something more to the friend and then finally goes up and takes her seat at the front of the classroom. In this class the kids always wait several seconds to do what the teacher tells them to do but he never reminds them twice. Sean, the "Metalhead" who had come in late with the excuse that he had trouble getting his pop out of the machine, takes his quiz up to the teacher with a loud sigh that I can hear from the back.

Teacher (looks over Sean's exam): You don't know anything else that shows up in an elevation drawing?
Sean: No.
Teacher (smiles in disbelief, pointing to the exam sheet): You don't know what that is? You don't know what this is?

The whole class can hear that Sean has left all these questions blank. Finally the teacher encourages him to go back down to his seat and write some more answers. Liz is up every five minutes, talking to the teacher, asking him questions about the exam. One boy sits at a chair so low that he can't work at the drafting table.

Teacher (after awhile): Okay, who's still writing?
Liz (back at her seat by now): I am.
Teacher: Well, there's a lot of talking going on if there's still writing. You're supposed to be thinking.
Liz: That's hard for me.
Teacher (shakes his head): No kidding. (then to her seat mate) Don't help her, Tom.

Liz then takes her paper up to the teacher and asks him more questions about the exam. Liz is standing at the podium side and the teacher is writing on her exam. A couple of students say, "Liz's cheating." Standing at the teacher's side she calls out "I'm not cheating. If I was cheating I'd have all the answers here!" The teacher really laughs at that. The teacher has to leave the room to get something.

Teacher: Watch Liz and make sure she doesn't cheat while I leave the room.
Immediately students start to shout, "She's cheating! Liz's cheating!"

After a moment the teacher returns and collects all the quizzes from chapters 16 and 17.

Teacher: Okay yesterday I gave you a paper for your final project. Who doesn't have theirs?

One of the "Metalheads" in the last row raises his hand. The teacher comes down and gives him one.

Boy 1 (about the "Metalhead"): He probably ate his paper.
Boy 2: Students don't eat paper.

Liz (to no one in particular): Curt (her former boyfriend) used to eat paper. He used to eat little tootsie rolls with the paper still on it. Put the whole thing in his mouth.

Teacher (ignores this): Draw a house to scale with 2000 sq. ft. for me . . . sometimes we draw houses in here and you don't have to keep in mind a budget and you're running up the cost of a house to $350,000–400,000 and no one's ever gonna be able to build it. Draw a house to scale 2,000 ft. for me within so much of a budget.

The four students with longish hair and baggy pants in the last row are not even listening. One reads a magazine. Three others never look up. A girl in front of them takes off eye makeup using a small bottle of liquid and tissues. The teacher goes on with detailed instructions on how to draw the floor plan. "Metalheads" keep banging their drawers in and out. The teacher draws a big rectangle on the board.

Teacher: I want to see dimensions written on the paper.

Ryan: Yeah. (as if to say yeah, yeah, we know.)

Teacher (raises his eyebrows and looks at Ryan and says slowly): I'm doing this Ryan, because I'm going to get papers without the numbers on them, without the rooms identified. Not everybody needs these instructions, but some people do.

After a while Liz comes to the back of the room and shows me her drawing of her house. She plans to put the garage on the roof over the bedroom. I say that would be very interesting. She asks the teacher a question about putting her garage on the roof.

Ryan: Liz, shut up.

Liz: You shut up, Ryan. I can talk if I want to.

Two girls, one of them removing the make up, look at each other as if to say, She's off today. Liz brings the Seventeen *magazine over to show me a picture of a gown that she got last year on sale. It's a red, fitted, Spanish-dancer type dress, short in front and long in back. She just hopes that she can fit into it because she's gained so much weight. I say, "When is the prom?" Liz says, "Sometime in April. I got this gown at Maurice's. I just hope nobody else has it." The bell rings and everybody dashes out.*

This class had so many competing elements it was amazing anyone could design his model home. It had late arrivals, soda pop drinkers, magazine readers, make-up removers, prom conversations, loud mouths (*"Yeah, Yeah"*), fashion plans (*"I hope nobody else has it"*), kids who were there but not participating, a teacher teaching (*"details . . . house plan"*) and of course, the ubiquitous Test (*"Anyone else still writing?"*) It also had a tendency of the teacher to make one of the few girls in the class the butt of his jokes (*"Make sure Liz doesn't cheat"*) and the victim of his sarcasm (*"It's hard for me to think." "No kidding"*). What this attitude of the teacher's did, it seemed to me, was give every boy in the class permission to undervalue Liz's presence and contribution there. And they did undervalue it (*"Shut up Liz."*) The boys in this class never got this kind of good natured-*sounding* attention from the teacher, as though their fringy status—earned by looking different from the class body—entitled them to gentle consideration: at least they are here, in school and not out plotting nefarious deeds. But Liz, who with her learning disability and prescribed anti-depressants certainly needed something special, gets to hear everyone have a laugh at her expense. And we wonder why a girl says things like *"Everybody knows I'm not that bright of a person."* Who ever tells her differently?

MYSTIFIED

"And I don't get the concept of anything."

Jenna, Grade 11

***

"The connexity of existence is the essence of understanding."

Alfred North Whitehead[16]

I once asked a psychologist who specialized in treating adolescents what he thought his patients would like to say honestly to their teachers if they had a chance. His quick reply, "They'd say, 'I don't understand. I never understand a thing you say to me.'" In fact, many students told me the same thing (*"I just can't catch it. It keeps going by me"*). The mystified student often turns to his plain-speaking peer for clarification (*"I'll ask this kid in front of me . . . he owes me for helping him in history . . . he'll just put it bluntly"*).

I think teachers assume if they don't hear questions from students, then it is safe to proceed. That is why it is so dismaying when we see generalized misunderstandings on a test. I would have been glad to clear this up! Why didn't they ask about that? We wonder depressingly what it is about our class that inhibits fruitful questioning. It is one of education's cruelest ironies that the student who needs clarification the most is the least likely to seek it (*"I've never seen anybody go up for help. Never, ever. People flunk tests instead of asking him. Rather flunk a test than ask him."*) At least a dozen times a period a teacher asks, Any questions? But a student response is uncommon (*"[the teacher will say] Well, did I answer your question? [You feel like saying] Well, no. But you just say, Yeah."*) Actually, if a student started to respond to the teacher's solicitation, I eventually could predict that his question would be about preparation for The Test. (There is little risk in asking about test requirements or expectations, in fact it makes you something of a hero: every shy test-taker in the room would send grateful vibes to you for that type of information.) What is it about the learning environments we create, that adolescent students do not feel truly empowered to blurt out, Stop, please. Help. Could it be that teachers are forgetting the age of their charges?

> Tim: He's above me. I don't think he knows he's talking to high school kids. He's very, very smart, I guess you could say, but just . . . He talks right over your head. He's a nice guy and stuff but he has us read books that are really hard to read. He likes them [sic] kinda books with a different type of talking. That's the way he does it: he just gets on a certain subject in the book, and you haven't read it, and you don't know what he's talking about. [But] he just goes on and on and on.

The students feel acutely the mismatch between the speaker's perception of his "audience" and their actual age and station (*"He's teaching us like we're in college . . . he's teaching us like we know everything that he's talking about."*) They forgive him for being so smart, in fact they expect their teachers to be smart (*"He's obviously read a lot more books than we have"*). But he should be smart enough to know the difference between a room full of seventeen year olds and speaking to a camera. The latter approach engages no one. Of course, many students admitted they do not do the assignment unless coerced by the threat of the test. Their social and work commitments are more urgent. The overworked teacher cannot be blamed for thinking that the ambitious student will meet him more than halfway (and the learning disabled will get help from the specialists). So he is doing his job. If the students in the middle choose to slough off, well it's their loss.

English class, September

> *Teacher (without a trace of irony): Cliff's Notes are not a substitute for reading the book.*
> *Student: Can we use them during the test?*
> *Teacher: No. I think it's a bad idea. I think they're poorly planned Cliff's Notes.*
> *Teacher: (begins* Scarlet Letter *discussion) My first period class wanted to read first and then discuss. What do you want to do?*
> *One student: Discuss first!*
> *Teacher: OK. Pearl . . . gorgeous child . . . what you would call a free Spirit . . . named because her mother paid a high price for her; knows she's different; from a single parent home. . . . One of the things that throws you as a younger person is how Hawthorne tries to recreate the dialogue of the Puritans. Let's look at p. 98. . . . She looks in her daughter's eyes and she thinks she sees evil. Incidentally, Hawthorne has created here a portrait of a mother who is not*

only concerned but adoring. It is not only her beauty but she is a child of in-
telligence, imbued with great intellect . . . indentured servants, early slaves,
nobody knows, but there is some belief that the early slaves were actually in-
dentured servants . . . has a Tudor house, made of stucco and wood, French
windows and a window seat . . . it is often taken as a mark of great achieve-
ment in America, even today . . . used utensils of pewter, mark of wealth, most
people used wooden utensils. . . DeTocqueville . . . tyranny . . . What happens
when you are a minority in America? (no answer) . . . (Hester's) single act of
passion . . . as a consequence she has a glimmer of what these people are in
a way that she otherwise would not have . . . Who is the father of Pearl?

Gene starts to answer, but does not. No one else does.

Teacher (does not tell them): Chapter seven is a very passionate scene . . . a
scene of love, great passion.

Many students look up for the first time.

Teacher: As you write these (chapter) summaries write things that will clarify
this information for you. . . . Let's get started everybody.

Joy and Annie are sleeping. Gene and Jesse are the only ones who have an-
swered. Gene volunteers his answers; Jesse is nominated to answer by the
teacher. "Discussion" is over; students start to read.

Teacher (interrupts): This is the vocabulary word for today: "labyrinth." (on the
board. Mentions it twice; does not give the definition.)

Gene: How old is the kid now?

Teacher: About three. Three years have passed.

Some students are working with the dictionaries.

Gene (abruptly): Why do they describe the characters so much in this book?
Teacher: Because it's all internal.

Gene looks like he doesn't get it.

Teacher (smiles): You know, if we wanted to describe you we'd go on for vol-
umes!

Gene: They'd say, "What a great guy!"

Students titter.

Girl: More like, about one sentence!

Two students leave for the learning disabled classroom for help writing chapter
summaries. Gene is now staring at his retainer, which he has removed from
his mouth.

We must note that the students ask for a discussion but their response to the
choice offered by the teacher is the last time we hear anyone's voice except
Gene's—and his is a factual inquiry. The "discussion" becomes a lecture in
very short order. Why don't adolescents feel like participating more? Is it the
archaic language of some literature ("*I know it's classics but it just doesn't re-*
ally interest people") that makes it unpopular with students? Is it the "arcane"

language of the teacher ("*labyrinth . . . indentured . . . imbued*") that makes it unintelligible to students? Or is it the dominant role of the adult that makes the students feel passive? Or is it all three? Would the level of participation from this class be any better if they were reading gothic novels instead of a selection from the great American literary tradition? Probably not: all our teaching tasks are formidable, given the competition from the slick symbols of the youth culture. To these teens, the arts and humanities must seem like a long, old fashioned, Sunday dinner: rich and filling—but who's got the time to relish its every flavorful nuance, let alone a recitation of its recipes? Students would forgive their teachers' quaint taste in literature; they are usually over forty, after all. What they do not get, is their teachers' anachronistic faith that today's teen would have read all of yesterday's assignment.

Studying literature can be a combination of aesthetic experience and morality lesson. Unfortunately for Mr. J, this tough class shields itself against fifty-five minutes of what feels like an assault on their heads. They have no interest in communicating about this book, unless it's a testable question (*"How old is the kid by now?"*) By their junior year, just about every single one of them has had a pregnant classmate.[17] But what could the shunned Hester Prynne possibly have to do with them?

English class, September

> *Someone snaps her gum. Mr. J begins by saying he will reverse the usual process and give them reading time at the beginning (not end) of class. Asks how many finished the novel (book is due tomorrow). No hands. One says, "I know so and so (who is absent) did!"*
>
> *Teacher: Hawthorn (in* Scarlet Letter*) is saying, "Look around you. We are not different." The issues have changed but there is still the issue of public vs. private. . . . For the people who were not here yesterday, taking a test, we did not spend any time yesterday on the chapter. . . . I'm going to give you about thirty minutes at the beginning of the period to catch up. You have a load of other assignments and many of you have fallen behind in the reading. So you can use this time to catch up. In this chapter, Hester looks for the first time into the eyes of the father of her child . . . Boston . . . Chillingsworth has chosen to live like a hypocrite; he has a darker purpose; he can willfully wreak his revenge. Hester lives with truth. . . . It gives her a keen perception on people she otherwise would not have. She is able to perceive the pain of others . . . Tapestry in Dimmsdale's room . . . David and Bethsheba . . . adulterous affair . . . Hawthorne wants you to know that a man who lives a lie has his perception and his intuition of others affected.*
>
> *Class regards him mutely.*
>
> *Mr. J starts the reading time. Many students do not even pick up the book, although not one said he had finished it. Josh is underlining in a textbook. Coral*

is sound asleep; never misses class but always sleeps. Girl next to John is looking through a tiny book. Another boy is holding up his copy of The Scarlet Letter *with one hand and filling out worksheet from another class with the other hand. Girl tells a boy after one warning look to stop rattling his keys. After a while, Josh is sleeping too. Sean rolls a pencil down his desk over and over. Amber turns around and looks at him with a disapproving smirk. The pencil noise can be heard all around the room, but the teacher ignores it. Annie sleeps. Joy is absent. Board says chapter summaries are due Friday.*

The teacher described above was well educated, holding a master's degree in his teaching area. He made continual references, using a rich vocabulary, to the socio-cultural context of the literature he assigned. But students complained about this, saying he confused them. Isn't it hard enough to keep track of what's in the *book* that you need to know, without all these extraneous details and new words?

NOTES

1. Dewy, John (1916b), "Learning as Experiencing," in Vandenberg, D., ed. (1969), *Teaching and Learning*, Urbana: University of Illinois Press.

2. "Authentic teachers respect their students, listen to them, create opportunities for their voices to be heard, and are open to making changes in their own teaching," in Brookfield, S.D. (1990), *The Skillful Teacher*, San Francisco: Jossey-Bass, p.164.

3. Henry, Jules (1963), *Culture Against Man*, NY: Vintage Books, p.159.

4. Students want teachers who recognize who they are, listen to what they have to say and respect their efforts. In classrooms where personalities are allowed to show, students respond more fully, both academically and personally." See Phelan, Patricia, Ann Locke Davidson, and Hanh Thanh Cao (1992), "Speaking Up: Students' Perspectives on School," *Phi Delta Kappan*, 73, 9, p.696.

5. 46% of students give low marks regarding the extent to which their schools have small classes with personal attention. The Shell Poll (1999).

6. "Robots teach almost all of my classes. My so-called teachers are for the most part unaware, unconcerned, and interested only in finishing all of the planned note-taking in the given 50 minute period. . . . School leaves me feeling confined and discontented," in: Gilbert, Robert N. and Mike Robins, (1998), *Welcome to Our World: Realities of High School Students*," Thousand Oaks: Corwin Press, p.49.

7. "But in every story I have heard, good teachers share one trait: a strong sense of personal identity infuses their work. 'Mrs. A is really there when she teaches,' a student tells me or 'Mr. B has such enthusiasm for his subject' . . . bad teachers' words float somewhere in front of their faces, like the balloon speech in cartoons," in Palmer, Parker (1998), *The Courage to Teach: Exploring the Inner Landscape of a Teacher's Life*, San Francisco: Jossey Bass, p.10.

8. Bateson, Mary Catherine (1990), *Composing a Life*, NY: Plume Books, p.37.

9. "Sensations of hearing and touch, sensations primarily attributed to the left hemisphere, develop earlier in girls while the ability to interpret spacial information, primarily attributed to the right hemisphere, develops earlier in boys," in Sousa, D.A. (2001), *How the Brain Learns*, Thousand Oaks: Corwin Press, p.175. Sousa also reports that boys between ages 6 and 12 will normally spend their time away from school in more outdoor activities where they rely more on space than time, are more apt to design their own games, use visual versus verbal skills and rely less on language.

10. Garbarino, James (1999), *Lost Boys: Why Our Sons Turn Violent and What We Can Do To Save Them*, NY: Free Press.

11. Gilligan, Carol (1982), *In a Different Voice: Psychological Theory and Female Development*, Cambridge: Harvard University Press.

12. Even when high-achieving girls reach college, they relinquish their long-held ambitions to enter careers traditionally dominated by men. See: Hoolan, Dorothy and Margaret Eisenhart (1990), *Educated in Romance: Women, Achievement and College Culture*, Chicago: University of Chicago Press.

13. See the American Association of University Women (1989), *Equitable Treatment of Girls and Boys in a Classroom.*

14. Myra and David Sadker (1994) suggest that standardized tests are written for the male population resulting in the female population being passed over in schools and business, and that this process occurs through subtle and overt gender bias in our classrooms: *Failing at Fairness: How Our Schools Cheat Girls.* NY: Simon and Schuster.

15. The school context does not provide a girl the opportunity to explore her position as a woman, consequently the school acts to promote the assumed dominance of white men. See Weis, Lois (1990) *Working Class Without Work: High School Students in a De-Industrialized Society,* NY: Routledge.

16. Whitehead, Alfred North (1938), *Modes of Thought*, NY: Free Press, p.32.

17. Thirty-three percent of North Dakota males (33% nationally) and 39% of North Dakota females (36% nationally) in grade 11 reported having had intercourse in the three months prior to a 1997 survey. Of those, 17% reported no use of birth control. In 1997, North Dakota (pop. 642,200) had 946 teen pregnancies and 759 live births among 12–19 year olds. Source: North Dakota Risk Behavior Survey, N.D. Department of Public Instruction, 1997. North Dakota ranks # 2 nationally in births per 1,000 females, 15–17 years of age. Source: *Kids Count Data Book,* 2000.

Chapter Five

Two Pathogenic As-Ifs

"Not many people at this age want to learn anything. We're rebellious. School is tedious."

Jennifer, Grade 11

***

"The aim of education is to produce a [person] of culture, that is, one who has a receptivity to beauty and humane thought."

Alfred North Whitehead[1]

In these days of skill-seeking and outcomes-obsessing, Whitehead's aim of education seems quaint, if not downright useless. Today, adroitness at the bottom-line, not receptivity to beauty, moves you up your career's ladder. Let's face it, you could be completely receptive to beauty and humane thought, and without some other "redeeming" aspect to your training many people in our society would judge you a failure. Whitehead's aim is about values; the modern public school structure is about drives. Jules Henry describes the difference:

> Fundamentally, values are different from what I call drives and it is only a se-
> mantic characteristic of our language that keeps the two sets of feelings together.
> To call both competitiveness and gentleness "values" is as confusing as to call
> them both "drives." Drives are what urge us blindly into getting bigger, going
> further into outer space and into destructive competition; values are the senti-
> ments that *work in the opposite direction.* Drives belong to the occupational
> world, values to the world of family and friendly intimacy. Drives animate the
> hurley burley of business, the armed forces, and all those parts of our culture
> where getting ahead, rising in the social scale, outstripping others, and merely
> surviving in the struggle are the absorbing functions of life. When values appear

95

in those areas, they act largely as brakes on drivenness. Though the occupational world is, on the whole antagonistic to values in this sense, it would nevertheless be unable to function without them and it may use them as veils to conceal its underlying motivations.[2] (emphasis added)

If we substitute the word school for the phrase occupational world we begin to understand why school feels so split along student/curriculum lines. Drives are what animate the hurley burley of school, where getting ahead, rising in the academic scale, and outstripping others are the absorbing school functions—as planned by adults anyway. Drives are the urge behind curriculum decisions: how will this course or that text prepare students for "surviving the struggle" in the occupational and political world—not: how will this or that make them receptive to humane thought. As a "drive," curriculum implementation grinds on and on. Like the giant federal bureaucracy during a national crisis, the secondary curriculum heaves itself forward, impelled by its own massive weight. And the curriculum does get heavier: in the 1950's the average number of courses offered in a typical Midwestern high school of 1000 students was approximately 22.[3] In the 1990's the number of courses offered in a high school of 1,000 students might have swelled to over 200,[4] layering new course over old. Now "Algebra II" is supplemented by "Child Care;" "American Literature" is supplemented by "Driver's Ed." It is an American cultural, political and inevitably, educational tenet that you never (nor should you try to) completely exhaust your choices. So the lists of curriculum offerings in a seven period day just multiply asexually, like coat hangers in the back of the closet. Some people like to point to the lists as evidence of progress. But real progress would include additional time for planning for the intersection of these new curriculum choices. Real progress would include equal commitment to improving instruction.

Someone asked a Wright brother why his new flying machine did not fall down. "Because, he explained, "it doesn't have time." The curriculum is much the same: it does not crash because the sheer momentum of the school day creates a little lift under its big creaky wings. The clock is always running. Teachers and students, who should be co-constructing the curriculum, cannot both get through the day *and* pause to reflect on it. Thinking about it would assuredly bring the curriculum enterprise to a full stop (teachers are hired on a separate contract to do it in the summer, when all other distractions are at bay). Meanwhile, during the school year, lists lengthen, parents persist, the world waits. The schools rush to ready the public's sons and daughters for college and for work, but completing this assignment has had its (to borrow a term from business) *downside*: a loss of personal meaningfulness for the student in the long and expensive career known as her education.

Values are different from drives. We could say values are what the students and teachers themselves bring to school. Values are feelings of worth that act as a brake on drivenness. As a consequence, teacher and student (the school community) can be said to be at cross-purposes with the public: where the public values competition, students and many teachers value collaboration; where the public endorses standardized tests, students and many teachers prefer specialized assessment; where the parent celebrates his child's independence, his child appreciates the shared *group* subculture. (The habits of the "group" are one major cause of friction between parent and adolescent. Doesn't every generation hear something like, "And if all your friends jump off the Brooklyn Bridge, will you jump too?" What makes parents think kids ever want to do *that*?)

If drives are what got us into space exploration, in response to a need to compete, it is the values people brought to the job which allowed them, in response to the need to cooperate, to get it done. Jules Henry is right: we require both drives and values. It is just regrettable that those in schools seeking a balance of these "sets of feelings" are regarded often as too sensitive, if not weak.

Over time, the consistent honoring of the value of humane thought in small ways will culminate in a positive school culture. For example, a teacher might have the habit of asking the class disrupter to meet her in the hall instead of berating him in front of everybody else, or she might take into consideration the crush of other homework before she assigns her own (*"You have a load of other assignments and many of you have fallen behind in the reading. So you can use this time to catch up"*). Just responding patiently to a multitude of personalities, month in and month out, the teacher teaches a respect for the individual. But in the general "hurley burley" of school, instances of humane thought are not remarked upon, as hundreds of people run through their crowded schedules, in crowded halls. (And it is crowded: the year I observed was the first time in a long while I had to make a quick choice between lining up for a drink of water and going to the bathroom. Since the teachers in these schools demanded a strict punctuality, the between-class five minutes did not allow time for both things, especially if the next class was on a different floor.)

In the class described below, a male math teacher deals subtly with the race issue as he facilitates the presence of two black students in a class that's about as white as the drift against the basement window. The class has its own drive, i.e., getting the homework done during the period so they don't have to take it home. But the veteran teacher attends to interracial peer involvement (a value), while his young student teacher teaches small group cooperation (also a value). As always, morality, Whitehead's humane thought, is instructed by silent example.

Math Class, February

The room has so few frills it resembles a university classroom. On the bulletin board there's a copy of a yellowed Ann Landers column that says,"Tough classes are worth the hassle." Next to that are biographical sketches of Isaac Newton and someone I've never heard of named Carl Frederick Gauss. The lunch menu is posted, and the fire drill procedure. There's a calendar of some sort on every wall: a big state Education Association poster that shows the twelve months of the year as August through August; school activities' calendars for February and March; a separate, small athletics' schedule. There's a long list of due dates on the board and next to every date, a math chapter. Virtually everything on the walls is a reminder of the passage of time. This is the year of retirement for this no-nonsense, but sensitive teacher, Mr. S.

On the board Mr. W has written "To err is human but when the eraser wears out ahead of the pencil you're overdoing it." The table where I sit has a built-in overhead but it's not in a place in the room facing a screen and it's kind of dusty so it's not used too much. There's a big green and blue globe on the table. Later I tell the teacher I thought it was an ecologically-correct globe, which really makes him chuckle; it turns out he uses it to illustrate geometry. He has a set of mailbox slots sitting on a table with about 20 openings; no mail in any of them. All the desks face front; the blackboard is usually filled right out to the edges. There are 18 kids in this class, 7 girls and 11 boys, scattered all over the room, and 11 empty seats. There's a floor fan in the room; looks out of place in February, but it's been very hot in here. The cooperating teacher of more than forty years of experience sits behind me; he's out of the student teacher's sight, and out of the sight of the class. The student teacher is teaching. She has seemed very tired lately; she took a night job waitressing in a bar to make ends meet. Both the cooperating teacher and the university supervisor had to tell her to cut back because she was so worn out. The cooperating teacher understood the financial stress, was sympathetic to her. To me he says, "You know, it isn't just the physical exhaustion but teaching is mentally exhausting too!"

The first assignment she gives the class is to problem solve for "a" and then write the solution in words. This takes about 10 minutes. Some people seem to find this harder than others. One girl asks her neighbor, a boy,"How do you do this?" He shakes his head, raises his shoulders and says to her, "When you figure it out let me know."

Student Teacher: Get into groups of two or three: three if there's an odd number. Do problem such and such, don't split [the problems] into steps, one taking one part and one taking the other. Turn your chair around, [or] whatever. Have your desk any way, I don't care.

boy: Do we have to do them in the [homework] assignment?

Student Teacher: No, if you finish them, you don't have to do them in the assignment.

A black boy stands up at the far corner of the class; he looks very hesitant, as if to say, Where do I go? Everyone around him has paired off. The cooperating teacher jumps up from behind me, sprints silently to the middle of the room, whips around a desk as if it weighs nothing, to face a white boy who is sitting alone. Mr. W calls the black boy over, puts a hand on his shoulder and says kindly, Sit here. The black boy moves without expression. He sits down. The white boy never looks up. The black boy and the white boy do not look at each other for five full minutes, nor do they speak to each other. Each of them is working on the problem by himself. The black boy writes continuously. The white boy starts to watch—the black boy's paper, not his face. The student teacher is circulating. As she comes by this "cooperative" pair she says gently, Are you guys okay? And they both say, Yeah. The student teacher keeps going around and bends over students who admit they need help. Sometimes, a teaching mendicant, she kneels right down next to a desk, kneecaps on the linoleum. Pairs of kids sit side by side; others face each other, trying to read their partner's paper upside down. After a few minutes the white boy says something and the black boy grins and then they talk a little bit, their eyes looking down in the direction of the other's work.

After a while a black girl enters the room late, from the office; she is joining the class in the middle of the period, in the middle of the year. The cooperating teacher runs right over and greets her warmly, as if this happens every day:"We'll get you working right here with these two girls." To the straight-A Tess and her partner (both white), he says politely, "Do you mind if she joins you?" The students do not look up but they reply together, "No, we don't mind." Again Mr. W moves a desk smoothly up to the pair so it's two white girls facing the black girl. The teacher moves on. After just a few minutes, future teacher Tess says amiably to the newcomer, "Here, move your chair around so you can see what we're doing."

In a long day in school, a class such as this had tiny authentic moments, observable even to a stranger, when humane thought was valued. The veteran teacher and student teacher were committed to the students as well as to the material. (The student teacher does have a way to go; her cooperating groups of two look busy, but they do not comprehend everything she is teaching.) Both veteran teacher and student teacher were aware of the students' presence, making them work together, while making sure they actually worked. They modeled to the students a genuine interest and genial acceptance. What was more typical in the three schools I visited were inauthentic moments—or to be more accurate, inauthentic hours—inauthentic because so many teachers and students did not seem connected to each other. Do most secondary teachers notice that students are inattentive? Do most secondary students even care that the teacher is up there trying to do a job? Teacher and students appear to be faithful to their roles, that is, each is doing what is expected of them. But in fact they are *disengaged*. Their "collaboration," which results in what we call a class, is not genuinely conjoined. Someone once said we live in worlds within worlds. He could have been describing the adolescent-world-within-the-teacher-world, the school's nesting Russian dolls. They are together in one place but they do not touch each other. Repeatedly, I was struck by the sense of futility of trying to teach this age group, with its distractions blinking like neon all around their heads. Every teacher was attempting to accomplish a lesson, often ineffectively, while at the very same time students were absolutely intent on accomplishing their own shifting (and shifty) agendas. Sometimes it was just sharing: news (*"She put her arms around my Sean"*); reading (*"It's about two upper bodies on one pair of legs"*); or a plan (*"I'm having three keggers."*) In every classroom I saw students carrying on conversations parallel to the teacher's talk (*"I know who was behind the grassy knoll—it was Elvis."*) They resort to (from the teacher's point of view) bizarre actions: sticking a pen in an electric socket, squirting a water bottle or wetting a rubber toy in their mouths so it would stick on a clock. They drink pop illicitly, roll their pencils down the desk, jingle their keys, pantomime a boxing jab to the shoulder, sneak a snack, braid their hair, remove make-up, apply make-up, rustle in their purses for an old note, hide the VCR remote, do their other homework, plot against a rival, daydream about their significant other while paying just enough attention to be on the page— if off the question. Sometimes the teacher required absolute dead silence in class, so news had to be shared quickly before the bell rang. If the news was dramatic—as it was the day a girl said to her arriving seatmate, "She was screaming at me, [saying] that I slept with her boyfriend. I did NOT sleep with him. That BITCH!"—it seemed to me impossible for storyteller or listener (or eavesdropper) to maintain an interest in the ensuing lesson. Little wonder the teacher drags their attention back to class with a test announcement.

To survive the onslaught, so to speak, of so much "irrelevant" information in school, the student believes she must derive energy from an entity apart from the teacher's agenda: a vivid interest, a keen sense of humor, *a relationship that counts*. As we say of much younger students, "They're on task. It's not the teacher's task, but they are on task." Teens are on the task of having a successful life at the moment they are living it. That involves much, much more than academic success; it involves a social success. And for that one needs an emotional buoyancy that the curriculum per se does not provide. Experience with one's peers provides it, eventually: compare the wide-eyed hesitancy of the nervous new freshman with the easy social equanimity of the seasoned senior. Gradually the latter has shed her heavy cloak of insecurity, riding out her high school years lighter and lighter with every passing month.

For the elementary level of teaching, where the sheer energy of the children demands periodic escape valves, we educate teachers to take the children's interests into account. The lesson should involve them, building on what they know to get to what they need to know (and they still need recess). At the high school level teacher and student seem to take less account of each other (*"In ninth grade they'd explain it. Now they're just figuring you know how to do it"*). Evidence for this mutual dismissal was the frequent and abrupt code shifting between teacher and student (*"[my boyfriend's] like, all the time, "Ohhhhh, I loooove you . . . How many questions is this exam Mr. S?"*) Their topics and tones did not conform to each other; their cadences of speech out of step. This is due to more than a difference in age or education. They are literally talking about different things, when in fact there is a chorus of their voices at all. The teacher would make a good faith effort to teach the abstraction, or assist them in constructing knowledge. Abruptly the student would say something incongruous, or tangential to the lesson. Like the parent and the five year-old walking slowly home from school that first Fall day: the parent says, "Here at the corner, we should look both ways for cars," and the child responds, "Hey! The leaves are chasing each other down the street." One has a heavy lesson to teach; the other her own light view of things. Whitehead would call it her "insistent present." The crossing lesson will have to be iterated again and again to make an impact. Do adolescent students let the teacher's message into their insistent present? In some classes better than others: I found that math, science and business seem less susceptible to student misapprehensions about the lesson. Everybody seemed to get it (that is, what it is they are expected to know) in those classes. The teaching typically turned back on itself, helix-like, to pick up the material needed for the next step. I think students pay a different quality of attention in those classes, perhaps out of plain old fashioned fear of being left behind (*"[In chemistry] we started building [on what we learned]. It's another "building" thing?"*) When they fail, and if they are honest, students assess themselves a share of blame for not studying. Whatever their academic success in math or science, students expressed much less fear of the "sneaky teacher out to get us." And by the way, there are fewer objections in those math and science classes to "teacher-talk." Where the information-delivery style of teaching might have a certain minimum value it is in those classes having a type of evaluation known by all to be straightforward. The expectations are clear and unambiguous: write down the assignment in your calendar, note the date it's due, get it done, pass it in, study it, and of course take the test. The classes might have been rather grim-looking, or in keeping with the thesis of this book, grim-feeling, but they came as advertised, that is, they consisted of information that students knew they would have to know at a later date. They were not bewildering as to their expectations. Not if you paid attention, anyway.

In the humanities it's different. For example, the teacher is conveying an important metaphor about "the end of the world" in *Yellow Raft Blue Water*[5] but as soon as he stops for a breath, the student wants to know if, on the worksheet, they should put one name under every category. The teacher raises an idea; the student gets right down to the nitty gritty. Over the year I would sit there thinking, this is pretty snappy stuff about Melville, Hawthorne or Fitzgerald. But the class would be shut down, silent. They regarded the teacher as if he were a bridge being built: it's something to look at, but they have no interest in *going* there. The Irish will say a topic is, "Fascinatin,' but borin.'" But for these kids it's not even fascinatin.' Fascinating is "I did *not* sleep with him!" Daisy Buchanan and Jay Gatsby? Who needs art, if art just imitates life?

For me as a class observer, it was like watching a group of people move silently around a dance floor to a very long song in their heads. The adult had a slow waltz in his head and the twenty-two teens had a hip-hop hit in theirs. Neither could hear the other's music. And since they were too polite to point out that their rhythms were mismatched (and not sure who should get the blame for it), they all *pretended that they were dancing to the same tune.* Furthermore, many parents would prefer the pretense; they don't encourage rebelliousness in their children these days (if they ever did). Maybe they get tired of cranky teenagers complaining of this teacher's freak-out or that teacher's monotone. Enough things of absolute wonderment and joy happen in these schools (more often as part of the extra-curricular activities) that it's easy for families to accentuate the positive: Be grateful you go to such a good school. Soon enough you'll face a real freak-out.

People act as if certain things about the educational experience were true when the evidence to support them is thin. Jules Henry calls this common tendency to pretend, "pathogenic-as-ifness."[6] For Henry, the human being is a natural dissembler: she acts as if she likes something when she does not, for example, greeting an enemy with a smile, or acts as if he believes something when he does not, for example, buying brand X toothpaste to improve his social life when he knows better. As-ifness in families becomes pathogenic when it has very negative implications for the mental or physical health of those involved. Pretending to others that you love your child while you deprive him of food at home would be pathogenic. School as-ifs become pathogenic when they inhibit the genuine learning that is the aim of education. In a year of close observations and hours of interviews I noticed two common school as-ifs: 1.) students acting as if the teacher were the enemy (s/he isn't); and 2.) everyone acting as if the important part of school were the lessons (they aren't).

TEACHER AS ENEMY[7]

"I think the teacher has at least a 40 to 50% involvement in how good a student does, along with the student's own interests."

Carson, Grade 11

***

"Whitehead was extraordinarily perfect as a teacher."

Bertrand Russell[8]

Not many of us teachers get the same review of our practice that the philosopher-mentor Whitehead received from his mathematician-student Russell. Whitehead was able to give his undiminished attention to his brilliant protégé, as the class was strictly a one-on-one tutorial. At the end of their turn-of-the-century collaboration, the two prodigious thinkers, teacher and pupil, delivered their seminal manuscript[9] to the publisher in a wheelbarrow. A continent away and four generations later, an American teenager would describe to me the Whitehead style, "[A good teacher] challenges you; but yet they'll sit and give you one on one help if you need it." A twelve-year school career develops students into connoisseurs of fine pedagogy: they will have spent fifteen thousand hours in school refining their taste by the time they finish. They know at least as much about watching teachers as they do of television, and of that they know plenty. Without spending a moment in a college lecture contrasting the mimetic and transformative approaches to teaching[10] students can address with ease the relative merits of teacher style. In an introductory teacher education class we can get a discussion going in about three seconds by asking, What characterizes good teaching? Students have been there; they have seen, and they *know*. And although they usually choose a teaching career in order to model their professional lives after people they admire, college students surprise us by claiming to be impelled to teach secondary by a poor teacher. They love their major subject, they'll say, and they want to teach it right. Teaching it "right" is apparently rather rare, by student assessment, and it falls on a continuum anywhere between good and great.

The good teacher is a clear and patient communicator (*"You don't wanna fall asleep."*) He does not obfuscate but instead "makes it almost 'everyday' talk, not just these big words." The good teacher "adds these little stories on the side." One popular math teacher makes his "esoteric" subject interesting by relating it to more prosaic endeavors (*"He explains how he uses his calculus skills in his farming, and figuring out how wide of an angle he has to put the sprayers on . . . it's really cool when he does that."*) The good teacher

is also fair, someone who evaluates students without comparing their per-
formances to each other, instead measuring their progress against their own
starting place. Students don't talk about the relative merits of criterion-based
and norm-based evaluation,[11] but they surely appreciate someone who tries to
understand them in their own terms:

> Laura: English. I had Mrs. C. this year. She was hard. But I liked it. I mean, it
> was a lot of fun. We'd have essays due, 800 words, the next day. I mean it
> would be a lot to cram in one night but she'd, like, go a whole week without
> an assignment and then you'd have an assignment that one night. I liked her
> . . . she was a fair teacher. She didn't grade everyone on a general basis. She
> got to know the person and then she knew what to expect from them. She was
> very fair. [by implying to us] you could've done better. She was really nice.
> She looked at the individual, what they could do. I don't do well in grammar
> but I can write. Write real well. See, I can't find my verbs and everything else,
> but I can write. She was really fair.

The *great* teacher is everything the good teacher is (clear and fair) but he
is also is strict, that is to say, he has high standards (*"He expected a lot from
us but he also made [us] teach"*). Students will moan and groan about the
level of work expected by teachers, (especially homework) but they appreciate the teacher who demands that they produce. The teacher who ignores the
sleeping student is the object of derision (*"She doesn't respect us and we
don't respect her"*). The great teacher won't stand for the sleepers (*"He
makes you think a little bit above your level"*). In fact the great teachers lay
down the law pretty concretely (*"He told me, 'Jerry, you're not doing your
work so, this week if you don't get all your homework done, I'm just gonna
kick you out of my class.' So I mean that was kinda a kick in the butt and that
got me to do my work"*).

Students object to teachers who will get on them but they understand that
it is often for their own good. They would rather have the attention of a strict
teacher than be ignored by a jolly teacher (*"He'll knock on the slackers and
everything to get them to try."*) There is absolutely no substitute for the feeling of sincere interest in your well being, even if the sincere interest requires
work from you (*"She wants people to do well. And for that reason it doesn't
make it quite as hard"*). The great teacher also empowers the student to reveal his ignorance in class without shame (*"You could ask a question in the
middle of a problem"*).

> Ross: About science: well, I had Mr. M last year for sophomore biology and he
> was great. Absolutely great, *great* guy. Cuz, he literally was strict. He kicked
> you in the butt. Oh! I mean we had 175 point tests. That's normal. Couple of

them a year. Oh, it was great though. And you know me: I'm not the type to take tests. But it was very interesting. And we just learned! We took notes and he'd talk about the things.

Interviewer: Really? But you said, he made you work real hard.

Ross: Yeah. He was real strict, in the fact that he wouldn't break down to students [when they were] saying, Oh, do we have to take this big huge test? Why is it so big? I mean we went through 200 bird slides. And we were tested on them. He cut out a chunk of 50 and pop em up there. We had to study! He'd scramble em up! Pop em up on there: what kinda bird is this? We had tests like that. Fish, wild animals, all kinds of stuff.

Interviewer: And when you guys whined, he didn't knuckle under.

Ross: He didn't knuckle under. He made us do it! And I'm glad he did.

Interviewer: Did it matter that he didn't act like he was your best buddy?

Ross: Right. Yeah. He did and he didn't. He was really good talking to, too. He really listened. Really listened. If you had a problem, he'd be a good guy to talk to. I mean he'd sit there and listen to you and he'd help you out. I mean anything. He was just . . . I didn't get super close to him. But I mean I know people who did. And I know he would've listened if I had a problem. You didn't have to be afraid of questions at all. I mean, in fact, it was when we didn't ask questions, he was a little concerned.

We recall that students feel neglected by teachers who cherish course content over community; but the great teacher is recalled long after graduation as "A good guy to talk to" (*"He talked to us if we had a problem or anything. He could see if something was wrong."*) Students respond to teaching that takes account of their "parallel life," the real one, the one that usually means more to them than the school life does:

Kevin: I always said, Oh I'm not going to take anything after biology. But I'm taking Chemstudy this year and I'm taking physics next year. I think it's getting to be more and more important to me. Cuz, like, our teacher this year, he really ties in a lot of things like with your life and how science plays a part. Chem*study*! I didn't think I'd have nothing [sic] to do with Chemstudy. . .he puts in little playful things sometimes. Like, how he talked about carbon monoxide poisoning and stuff like that. And how *parking* ["romantically"] has an effect on it. And like we were talking about alcohol and really it's yeast urine. He told us all if we wanted to go out and get drunk we could go around and follow our cat around or something.

Interviewer: Follow your cat around?

Kevin: For the urine! Cuz that's all that alcohol is. We're like *okay*. But I mean he does little stuff like that so . . . it's kinda neat.

Mr. A. is a Spanish teacher who was considered great: so strict no one dared sleep, informal enough that students joked around in class, and yet very sensitive to their apprehensions. Above all, students knew that the tasky Mr. A truly wanted them to succeed:

Spanish class, January

There are posters of Mexican towns hanging on the walls. As usual there are 4–5 kids around the teacher's desk when the class begins. Although Mr. A himself does not smile very frequently, the kids tease him. All the kids call him senor; the tone in the class is very informal. The kids ask him about his plane departure to Spain. Will he be in class in the morning? Mr. A nods. The kids all joke about having a send-off at the airport for him. They are very relaxed, lots of good-natured kidding back and forth. Finally everyone in their seats, Mr. A says "shhhh" several times, trying to get the class started. He calls out a student's name to bring his attention to himself. Finally everyone's watching the teacher. His voice is very deep and commanding; he has a really fine Spanish accent. This class has daydreamers but never sleepers. Mr. A begins by discussing a test that he's corrected and he's very upset with the results:

Teacher: Because when everyone does horrible on a quiz I feel like I should get a different line of work. I don't think I could've done better in preparing you guys. I did [this]. . . I did [that]. But half the battle is in [your] determination!

Then he reviews the exam. He calls on a boy who had done very poorly in the exam.

Teacher: What's the answer to number ten?
Boy (sarcastically): Like I got it right.
Mr. A does not laugh. Class chuckles and he calls on Angie.
Angie: I don't got it
Teacher: So you don't HAVE it?

Next the class recites vocabulary in unison. It's a lesson on personal grooming: tooth brushing, hair combing, dressing and bathing. Victor, a boy in the last row, calls out almost every answer. At one point he asserts, "I should get extra credit for that, Senor!"

A student says, "What page are we on?" Mr. A frowns and says "Mama mia." Next he reads vocabulary words; he tells the class to write them down. The boy in the last row, last seat, Ben, is sitting motionless.

Teacher: Ben, are you writing these down?
Ben: Yup.
Teacher: Where?
Ben: Here.
Teacher: I don't see a pen.
Ben (with annoyance): I just started.
Teacher: Okay.

Mr. A goes on with the vocabulary, using flashcards, translating into English. He tells them that in Spain people have a very different attitude towards trash and if they want to throw something away they just let it go. . .

Teacher (interrupts himself): Okay Betsy, do you want to go to your regular place?

Betsy: I'm not even talking!

Teacher: Okay (goes on with the lesson.)

The girls don't move. Later Betsy (who objected to being reprimanded) will say, "'Vamanos:' is that going to be on the test?"

Teacher: No, it's so similar to vamos that I put it on the board so you wouldn't get confused.

Mr. A goes through all six new vocabulary phrases over and over again, making the class repeat for pronunciation practice.

Teacher: Okay, get into your groups and ask each other the 7 questions on page two hundred. I want to hear nothing but Spanish. Get into your groups, I want to hear nothing but Spanish chatter.

The girl passes a paperback (not a Spanish book) to an adjoining group. To the girl taking the book she says, "It's about two upper bodies on one pair of legs. Really cool." Some kids move their desks in such a way that they can actually talk to each other. In the back of the room what seem to be two groups of three and four are all massed together so it's hard to see where one group leaves off and the other begins. In one group, girls are not talking to each other at all and one is writing in the book. Off to my left a boy and a girl aren't talking at all and one girl is writing. Mr. A is at the desk asking by name for kids to come up and demonstrate to him that they've completed assignments in their workbooks, after which he will enter a grade in his grade book. The kids do not seem to hear him. He calls out six or so names in a row. No one moves.

Teacher (finally exasperated) Okay, I'm going to put all zeros and close the book. I'm not going to beg for workbooks.

Kids start to move and run up. After a while Mr. A passes out a collection of papers that he's put together for the students so they can review for their exam the next day. One boy stands up and walks to the front because he has three empty desks in front of him to get two papers being passed back to him. When he comes back to the girl who sits behind him he teases, "Which one should I give you?" with a little smile. The girl laughs and says, "Either one."

Next Mr. A has everyone read from the workbook sentences in Spanish. Some of their pronunciation is atrocious. When he's calling on them for this vocabulary exercise he shuffles cards on which everybody's name is written, their actual name and their Spanish name. They never know when their name is going to be called. Ben seems like he's daydreaming, maybe even asleep. When he is called on he reads the wrong sentence in the book. Someone titters and then Ben says defensively, "I was only ahead one." Some of their responses are so mumbled that you can barely hear them. Mr. A never actually corrects them, he just repeats the phrase in beautifully accented Spanish and says, Muy bien, no matter how poorly they do.

Teacher (kindly, in the middle of all of the repetition): The number one fear is speaking in public, even worse than death.

Shane has taken Tom's honeycomb which is a plastic toy that sticks to a surface if the suction cups are moistened, and when Mr. A was occupied elsewhere, Shane has stood up on his chair and quickly attached the honeycomb to the center of the clock. It's sort of sticking out there, about as big as a hand. Mr. A ignores or does not see all of this. Then, just before the bell rings to end class, Mr. A comes down and pulls the honeycomb off.

Teacher: Who does this belong to?
Tom: It's mine.
Teacher: How did it get on the clock?
Tom: Well, I'd rather not say, but I didn't do it.
Teacher: Well, I'll have to throw it away.
Tom: Senor . . . But, Senor
Boy: Oh Senor, how can you touch it? It's been in everybody's mouth. It's full of saliva.

Mr. A never stops. He's breaking off the suction cups and we can hear the plastic splitting. Now the whole class has filed out. As I leave, Tom is standing in front of him protesting.

Tom: Senor, it's my honeycomb. I didn't even put it on the clock.
Teacher (tries again): Where did you get it?
Tom: Senor, it was a present from my teacher in second period.
Later I meet Tom in history and he says, Hi. I say, Did you get your honeycomb back? He shrugs, Nah, he threw it away.

This class had a little bit of everything: my year of observing in microcosm. It had a conscientious teacher who cared about the students' progress, who incorporated several different approaches to the lesson within fifty-five minutes, like a pitcher with a repertoire of change-ups. It had kids flirting with each other, conversations paralleling the teacher's talk, references to The Test, encouragement for all ("*muy bien*"), punishment for the class clown, recognition of the students' plight ("*fear of public speaking*") In short, it was multi-layered in its complexity: the class insisting on its own identity, and the teacher patiently pulling their attention back to himself, over and over again. He was teaching them Spanish. But he wasn't the enemy.

All the students I interviewed could recite inventories of their abilities, as though they had been flies on the wall for eleven years of parent/teacher conferences. They described "natural" learning and failing tendencies that seem beyond mortal influence to change. They spoke glibly, and as usual, emotionally, of subjects that had *always* been their "good" ones ("*I love History; I think I have a fetish for the past*"), or their "bad" ones ("*Math is just NOT something I can get along with*"). I asked them to order cards with the names of the curriculum's subjects, from their best (favorite or highest grades) to worst (least favorite or lowest grades.) I could tell from the moment they started which way the learning pattern was going to go: if math was the favorite ("*I always do good in your algebra's*"), English was on the bottom, with History close behind. And vice versa. This was true across all grade point levels: a student who was a perfect 4.0 could say, I don't like math; I *get* A's but unlike English, I have to work at it. Along with their assured oral self-assessment, students described a chronic, mild bitterness where it came to their teachers, who got a hefty share of blame, we recall, for their failures. Not all teachers, all the time, but frequently enough that "Teacher-As-Enemy" was the salient pattern of their interviews—just ahead of their celebration of "Friends-As-Salvation."[12]

Reviewing students' feelings about school (Chapters 2, 3 and 4) we see that they felt coerced, bothered and bewildered by their teachers and peers. Young moral relativists, they resisted the implication that they must adopt the ideas of the teacher in English or History classes. They thought English is "only reading, not right or wrong," so they are annoyed that there can be any essay marked low. To be fair, this attitude of feeling coerced was most often revealed by students who admitted that their best subject was not English. Possibly they were graded lower than classmates due to other factors: a lack of writing skill to present their ideas cogently; or a careless organization which conveyed a disregard for the whole exam enterprise. Maybe they were not graded down for disagreeing with the teacher, but simply because they just were not clear and convincing writers when it came to their own ideas. But why didn't they understand their deficiencies better? And why didn't they understand the requirements of cogent presentation? With all the relentless evaluation going on in these classes, doesn't everyone have a right to an explanation of what they need to do to improve? I believe the reason the strict-as-stone Mrs. E (Chapter 2) is so idolized by her students is because she spends a lot of time, one on one, describing what they have to do to improve. Students will not always seek teachers out for an explanation when they receive a poor grade even if they know it was a teacher mistake in calculating. A fear of approaching the teacher prevents them from saying, My tests did not add up to this. So they just accept the [unjust] grade and keep on going.

A more persuasive case for being "coerced" in English classes was made by excellent students who felt the "trivial pursuit" game was overplayed in testing. They preferred (because they wrote well) essay assignments; they resented the teacher's constant checking up on their progress with tests on "things that don't matter." The possibility that teachers might test on specific items to give the poor writers a chance to do well does not occur to them. In any case, the amount of resentment around English class testing and teaching, by all caliber of students, was significant. (As an observer in many different classes, I always sat in the back where I could see the most, and where I saw many disruptive activities on a regular basis. I myself enjoyed many of the lectures in subjects I had long forgotten and, neglecting my job of observing students, often had to force my attention back to them.) But in every subject the threat of testing was used to bring student attention to where the teacher needed it to be (*"I will give a test on this movie and it will count AS A REAL TEST."*) If they could not do the oral assignment it was converted in an instant to a written one (*"Let's make it a quiz, then."*) Does the teacher think that they get their synapses firing faster with pens in their hands? Students tell us that the test threat does not work to make them learn it better. I think the test threat makes them connect learning to punishment. And it reinforces the idea of the teacher as enemy.

Teachers having "pets" also made the students construe them as the enemy. This phenomenon was unexpected, not just because kids believe teachers have certain individuals whom they prefer to others and not because most of the time these "pets" are perceived to have a certain income level or athletic success. I was surprised that even students across low and average ability levels thought you had to *be* a pet to get a good grade; that they had to make a certain personal compromise to advance. In an unusual attempt at circumspection, teens hated the pets who had an easy rapport with the teacher, yet they "understood" that sucking up was what it took to do well (*"You hafta let her know you want the A, you don't want the B."*) Students simply do not appreciate the teacher who has a recurring conversation, whether it's sports, theater, or jokes, with a subset of the class (*"It's like we're not a group."*) Incidentally, there was no sense from students that the teacher, in the middle of a crowded but lonely day, might appreciate a refreshing conversation with a student who can bring in a new story or humorous anecdote. It's the pattern of it that offends: students perceive the persistent "junior discussants" as favored, able to get away with more by doing less. So the whole enterprise gets turned on its head: instead of being applauded or envied, the "favored" (recipients of undue attention and unearned grades) are regarded with cynical contempt by their peers. But it's the teacher who is the real enemy—for falling for the suck-up in the first place.

Another way the teacher becomes the enemy is to yell at students at the drop of a hat. The evidence for this yelling was pretty thin, although the tone of the teacher's voice can convey a powerful disapproval (*"See me after class."*) In the stingy reward system of the school, the teacher's smile and gaze are overvalued. So if they are withheld, and the words and manner suggest a reprimand, the effect of the "punishment" is exaggerated as well. The students call it being busted. We learned further that we should not underestimate the strong affiliation students have for one another, so that if one's friend gets the riot act read to him, he feels it acutely himself. I was struck by the silence and stillness that descend on a fidgety room whenever someone received the teacher's disapproval. Is that why she does it? Does she hope all would learn the one lesson by doling out a single public reprimand—a seeping spillover of repentance and resolve? We hear the story of the director Orson Welles who, at the start of a new movie, would hire one person— intending to fire him from the set on the first day—thereby putting everyone on notice as to who was the boss. The teacher probably does intend to put all future rule-breakers on notice at once. But in the end the offending student doesn't get the reputation as a rule breaker. More likely, the student gets the reputation as put-upon, and the teacher gets the reputation as punitive.

The enemy-teacher is seen to have no real interest in the student. We saw in Chapter 4 that students report feeling neglected by the teacher (*"You don't feel like she'd care if you had a problem. So you don't communicate with [her]"*). The enemy teacher is unconcerned whether or not the students are sitting in their seats listening (*"He wouldn't explain it to us at all . . . he wouldn't talk to us at all"*). Students said teachers only want to explain the material to those who don't *need* the explanation (*"And if you ask him a question he takes it offensively"*). Students saw as an enemy the teacher who teaches the material without noticing their boredom, restlessness, or commitment to their relationships. The chatty teacher (*"Every hour is just him, talking"*) is not exactly the persecutor that the "pop quiz" giver is but he is still a type of enemy because he mystifies, obfuscates, relays ideas without regard for age and station (*"I think he should be teaching college."*) This is what professors do; they carry on, not noticing much if someone is an eighteen-year-old freshman or sixty-year-old senior. They cover the material. And of course, most college students do not invest energy in regarding the professor as the enemy (except—and this is significant—just after exam time, when the occasional professor has been known to be in mortal danger from a disappointed student, fresh from twelve-plus years of grade-obsessing). In the college setting, neither "side" takes any real notice of the other, save for those majors where a certain personality type is helpful for a successful evaluation: counseling psychology say, or teacher education,. High school is different, not just because in high school teacher and student spend more time in each other's company—5 hours per week for 9 months in high school vs. 3 hours per week for 4 months in college—but because the responsibility of high school teacher to student is encumbered with the parents' expectation of a tender regard for their children. The parents want the teachers to see them holistically, so they can grade them individually. Their children know this too, which is why they speak with bitterness of teachers who "don't seem to care if you're there," or who stereotype them in terms of their gender.

Students act *as if* the teacher is the enemy but I believe they themselves are a type of enemy: to the teacher, through their indifference to the curriculum. Such indifference is a hardly a crime; adolescents just have little interest in meeting the teacher halfway, as the competition for their attention from other quarters is quite intense. But rather than take responsibility for their own indifference, for choosing to locate the majority of their attention elsewhere, students construe the teachers' efforts to deliver the curriculum as intrusive, if not oppressive. And this perception is widespread across interests and ability levels. Even really hardworking students who are ambitious, and faithful to the assignments, have a noticeably flat affect when discussing school, unless it is about their extracurricular activities[13] or buddies. I believe this is the case for two reasons: first, because most of the teaching and curriculum I saw added up to a drab and draining day, and second, because the teen culture requires students to perceive their school experience in terms of two dichotomous groups, one in authority over the other, a them-against-us. I believe that while school is no bargain, neither is the teacher the hate-filled enemy. He is not out to get them or trying to defeat them. He is not sneaky or plotting. (There's precious little energy left for that kind of evil endeavor, even if he were inclined, which seems unlikely.) He is merely, but demonstrably, guilty of retreating into a sterile subject-centeredness. So what feels to the student like being oppressed by an enemy is really a battle joined by both sides, the one teaching carelessly and the other resisting assiduously being taught.

LESSONS AS THE IMPORTANT PART OF SCHOOL

"I'd rather be homeless than lonely."

Sunny, Grade 11

***

"[In all of nature] there is no possibility of a detached, self-contained local existence."

Alfred North Whitehead[14]

Our local existence, as Whitehead calls it, is defined almost completely by our family when we are young. Until we are about eighteen, we depend on our parents for housing, health care, nutrition, transportation, safety, clothing, fun, information, education, socialization, *affection*. In the teen years the peer group begins to shoulder many of these agencies, thereby dividing adolescent loyalties between the old guard and the vanguard. For many adolescents there is no contest at all, as the peers inexorably become the company of choice.

Then, as one seventeen year-old boy confided to me gravely, "Having a family is a *real* problem."

Independence from adult supervision at this age is not a modern Western tradition by any means. Anthropologists report adolescents' "natural moratorium" on family attachment (more commonly by boys) as a cross-cultural phenomenon.[15] They describe a wide variety of living arrangements for adolescents in cultures all over the world. Separate sleeping community dormitories (not households) for boys and girls are seen in societies in Africa, southern Asia, and the Pacific. The Murias in India and the Nyakyusas in Tanzania dispatch adolescents to a village of their own, attached to their parents' village, where they live together, farming and keeping animals. Hopi boys will frequently sleep in the *kivas* or ceremonial buildings used as men's houses. In fact in any society that has ceremonial housing for men who are widowed or divorced, or sleeping away from their wives for some reason, adolescent boys will often choose to sleep there. In the Middle Ages the practice of child fosterage, in which children were apprenticed to noble families as pages was common. And "loaning out" or "farming out" adolescent boys for labor continued right into this century in both Europe and America.

Anthropologists, sociologists and psychologists may differ about whether peer affiliation is the cause or consequence of parental "separation." What is true in our culture is that adolescence is that unique life period when we are too old for supervision by adults and yet are too young for responsibilities of our own. Small wonder that in this existential limbo the psycho-dynamics between teens and parents can be so, well, *active*. And although it was not unheard of for students to say, shaking their heads for emphasis, "I tell my mom everything," or "My mom knows everything about me," most would agree that, "Friends are important to turn to when you need to talk." In response to a question about what was important, students mentioned family, friends and education, in varying order. Many students had the same answer, though the name changed with the individual: "Important to me? [They'd say] My best friend Kristi!" (Or Todd or Beth or John.)

> Thea: What's important to me? My boyfriend's important to me. And my friends. And my family. If I had to list them I think I'd go, most important to least important, would be right now, probably my friends, then my boyfriend, then my family. Which isn't really nice to say but [I say this] because it's not like my family can listen to me as well as my friends and my boyfriend can. I'm not like one of those kids at school that has like a million ten friends. I have like three really good friends. Tanya, Ellen and Devon . . . they're really great. They're always there for me. I don't know. Even if they don't believe in something that I'm doing, they'll stand by me.

In all our conversation students were the most animated when describing their friends, as though the intensity of the adolescent bond were in inverse relationship to its duration. The egalitarianism that marks their friendships as teens (*"She's almost identical to me; she has the same problems in school!"*) will be replaced by eventual differences in career choice, responsibilities, location, ambition, income, luck. For now, fun and steadfastness (*"You can be 95 years old and he or she will still be there!"*) are the cherished characteristics in The Other. The friend knows what you need: s/he gives you a ride, gives you the answers, gives you grief for going back to a bad relationship, shares homework, opinions, predictions. The friend will lend you clothes, money, make-up, accompany you to the mall, to the doctor, to the interview, or on the repeated drive by the house of the ex, or future, significant-other. The friend will pitch in for the gas, for the beer, or with help on the shoveling so you can both get going. The friend will call to see if you made the team, find out if you're going to be invited, ask around to see if that person likes you. The friend keeps your secret, gets you home when you're wasted, forgives when you forget your father's plan for your life. The friend's existence has a seamlessness with your own (*"My friends like me because they see a little part of themselves in me. And I do, them!"*) Above all, the necessary role a friend plays is as listener, because s/he's easy to talk to (*"You can tell friends how you feel."*) And the capacity to absorb others' feelings seems boundless: even after spending hours together out someplace, the teenager will instruct the driver as she gets out of the car, "Call me as soon as you get home." Years later some of them will pay a hefty fee for an hour of the same kind of sounding board. But for now their low budget therapists are their peers. The highest compliment they can pay is, "S/he's always there for me." Several students indicated their friends did not always approve of their choices or behavior but "stood by" anyway. Ironically—because they prefer peers' parallel lives to parents' protection—adolescents return home for an analogy for friendship, exclaiming in interview after interview, "Friends are like family!" Perhaps they mean that friends are like the family they used to have, because once they have left childhood behind, adolescents cannot, or will not, discuss with their families the things that have begun to preoccupy them.

When Christine's romance ended she was so depressed she actually has no memory of Christmas that year. Her friends and the school addiction counselor rescued her. Chris's relationship with her mother had changed too much for her to seek solace there:

Christine: During the school year from last June till—was it till after Christmas time?—anyway, I was going out with this guy named Nick for seven and a half months. And when we broke up, I felt terrible. I felt so alone and empty and stuff and I went through counseling and stuff and I realized. I finally got myself back on my feet. It was horrible. I couldn't believe how attached I get to people. Really fast. It was a shock, I guess. And I think I went crazy and lost my mind for a while.

Interviewer: Did you? Was it because he went to someone else?

Christine: Yeah. I think that was part of it. Um. And it was just such a change from not, not feeling loved I guess. And stuff, so.

Interviewer: Did he go to your school?

Christine: Yeah. He graduated this year from Madison, so that made it a lot harder, seeing him in the halls.

Interviewer: Oh yeah.

Christine: So I felt like I really lost something there but . . .

Interviewer: Who helped you through that?

Christine: Um, Mrs. C.

Interviewer: Oh, great. And did your sister help? Or your mom? Or was it not the sort of thing you could talk over with them.

Christine: Well, I used to be able to talk to my mom about that but now I don't know. I guess she's changed and I'm changing and so we aren't as close as we used to be. And [my sister], she just really disliked Nick. She never wanted me to have nothing [sic] to do with it. So she wasn't happy . . . she wasn't there to lend a shoulder or anything. But [the counselor] was, and Barb and a lot of my good friends, so. [They] helped me through it.

Interviewer: That's good. Would you advise girls who are juniors not to get too attached? Is that a lesson you learned? I don't want to put words in your mouth.

Christine: No. Yes. Um, I advise that you never . . . I mean this is only high school. You're here! Don't focus your high school years with one person, you know. See a lot, [see] many people. Be with your friends a lot. That's one thing I regret doing. I kind of dropped my friends for 7 months and just was with one guy. Cuz once you lose them then you really don't have anyone to turn to. It's hard for a lot of girls I know. It was really hard for me not to get attached. I get attached very quickly.

We would not recognize every teen who is in despair (*"From the outside, people think I'm really cheerful."*) but the statistics tell us we should be more vigilant. In North Dakota, suicide was the third most common cause of death (12.2%) among adolescents. The teen suicide rates here are slightly higher than the national percentages: 22% (21% nationally) of teens between grades 9 and 11 have considered suicide, 18% (16% nationally) have planned it and 10% (8% nationally) have actually attempted it.[16] If they have contemplated suicide they told me it is their friends who are more likely to have noticed (*"Friends are literally the life support of you"*). Even if their preoccupations were merely stressful, teenagers depend on the friend more often than the family (*"We tell each other . . . about any problems"*). In open-ended conversations some would refer lightheartedly to their depression (*"What's important*

to me? Getting through high school alive. Alive, and with some sanity left.")
And two students (both girls) chose to discuss their own emotional problems,
one showing me matter-of-factly the healed scars on her wrist.

> Interviewer: Do you feel like people don't understand the pressures you're under?
> Sandra: I mean, they should, they must know that we have our little problems
> like everybody else. But sometimes, it's hidden and they, especially don't
> know it. . . I think a lot of teenagers would rather keep it quiet than talk it out,
> you know? There's some people who can't say it, but, they don't want to talk
> to people. They just want to drop hints, so they can get help. Everybody wants
> help once in awhile in their life. If I wanted help, I [would] have to pull my-
> self through things, you know? My mom didn't care. . . Inside I'm totally hor-
> rified. I have so many stresses. And that's what it is to be in high school, I
> mean, for this day and age, there's more stressful things that people think
> about. And then . . . I don't think people give enough teenagers credit, or be-
> cause, um, they're working, everybody's concerned about their grades and
> their teachers. Everybody. It doesn't matter if you're a Head Banger, a Preppy
> kid, a Druggie, everybody is concerned. Even if they're trying not to show it.
> And, they're concerned about how they will be in front of their friends. A lot
> of it is peer pressure . . . that's why a lot of people drink. That's why I drink,
> drank, whatever. And that's why I smoke . . .

Another girl discovered a lockermate's suicidal intentions. It is significant
that Trish turned first to her friends before any adult in the building to handle
the emergency:

> Um, I had a really hard school year last year. A friend of mine and I shared a
> locker . . . she's a very close personal friend of mine but . . . when she was
> [younger] her father died. And it was really hard for her because . . . she
> wasn't told by her mother. She was told by someone else that she didn't know,
> who was over there that morning. It was a really hard death for her to take be-
> cause her parents had just separated and her dad meant everything to her
> . . . he's the one who taught her how to skate. Last year I was going through
> my locker trying to find a notebook and I saw this note written to me in one
> of the notebooks. And it was like a 3 page note. And of course I looked at it.
> And it was written by her. And it was a suicide note saying good-bye. I was
> so lost. I walked around school and I mean Ron was there to help me and Jess
> was there to help me. I didn't know what to do. I didn't know if I should take
> it to the counselor or if that would screw up her life too much. What I ended
> up doing . . . I took it to the counselor and then they weren't gonna get a hold
> of her till 6th hour. This was like 3rd hour. I had to go to lunch with her and
> I had to sit through class with her. They said not to say anything, cuz she
> might take off and run, you know. She might not want to be confronted by it,
> about it by her parents and other things. And I went to lunch and I tried to be

as cool and casual as I could around her and I cried during every one of my other classes. And I just . . . it was really hard. And then I went to 6th hour and she had taken off. That means the counselor had called her and she was at Dr. G.'s office. And she got back and she was in the counselor's office and I got this note for me to come down there. I went down there. I mean if looks could kill, I would've been dead. And I wanted to say I was sorry. But I wasn't sorry for what I had done! I knew that I had done the right thing. And she looked at me with questioning eyes. And she opened up her arms and she hugged me. And we cried and we cried. I mean from there on out we've been through a lot together. We've made it through a lot of things. She's the all American girl: the blond hair, blue eyes. She's very pretty. She gets along with just about everybody. I'm not that way. I mean I get along with a lot of people but I'm not this raving beauty like Carol is . . . she's got so many friends and she could be friends with so many people yet her [sic] and I have remained close through all of this. And I mean, I knew she had attempted it before. Suicide. Several times.

This story, told a year after it occurred, is as fresh in this student's mind as if it were yesterday. The idea that she was expected to go on through classes and lunchtime without showing her worry to Carol seems unrealistic. Did anyone notice she cried all through the rest of her classes? We have no way of knowing but I expect not, as I witnessed several students on various occasions weeping silently into their hands and never once saw a teacher take them aside for consolation. All it takes to be aware of such a situation is to *look* at them in the course of the period. It's true that secondary teachers do not get an education in counseling, and their students can be experiencing significant losses. But is it too much to expect that a teacher would suggest to the student in the hallway that she go to the counselor's office for the duration of the period? What the students chose to confide there would be a different decision, but at least an adult would have noticed her personal difficulty. Instead, it's the friends who take the time, risking reprimand by passing notes of encouragement.

In school the vital function of friends is to relieve the tedium of the day. Pity the poor home schooler: where are the pals who will lift the day up with the joke, the news, the *inclusion?* The fanciest curriculum innovation a teacher could design pales in importance next the friend's bright presence there (*"One of the best things about school is coming to see your friends"*). Friends compel attention, inspire devotion, give you a pleasure success cannot (*"All the money in the world will not buy you the happiness a friend can give"*). Friends—not a thirst for knowledge—impel an early recovery to go back to school. You might take Monday to be "sick," but you would drag yourself half-dead to school on Friday, the day when everyone is making week-end plans. "The best part of school is interacting with people," the straight-A Mark says matter-of-factly. Choosing between Calculus II and trigonometry? No problem for Ellen: "I go to classes where my friends are." Typically, a great class in a despised subject is due to the presence of the friends ("*We had a great math class last year [because of] the people that were in it. We did not pay attention*").

Educators claim smaller classes are better learning environments.[17] Students tell us why: "A small class, they explain, "is like talking to your friends." Far from being an adult-directed enterprise where kids develop cognitively—and then happen to find peers there to interact with—school for adolescents is the reverse. School is the center of their thinking and feeling because that is where their peers are. And they might happen to learn there too. "High school is our life, sums up Sara, a future teacher, "but it's not the classes. It's all the branches that come off of high school." To be relationship*less* in the driving wind of the school environment would leave you silently shivering ("*People constantly make it sound like [what is important is] school. Well, it's not! Music's not even the most important thing. Theater isn't. It's relationships!*") Being with friends mitigates their hurt at getting "drilled." Being with friends helps them, in fact requires them, to shrug off teacher neglect or school-subject mystification. People's painful memories of high school are of feeling excluded from the school's mainstream culture, not from being excluded from the National Honor Society. People's warm memories of high school are from being included with friends' good times and heartaches. That is why it will always weigh more heavily when one's friend fails to meet expectations than when a teacher freaks out:

Chemistry Class, April

Teacher (frowning): Jeff, will you be here tomorrow?
Jeff: No.
Teacher: So you'll take [the test] today?
Jeff: I've been gone for three days (meaning he has missed most of the work to be tested).

The whole class reluctantly eavesdrops.

Teacher: Do you have anything for me?

Jeff shakes his head.

Teacher (drops his chin, eyes level): You have nothing?

Jeff blinks.

Teacher: See me after class.

Jeff's friend, who sits next, and lives next door, to him, pats his shoulder as if to say, It'll be okay. Jeff is pale, he looks unhappy about this public reprimand about not having three days of homework to pass in. But after a few minutes he says to his neighbor, "Did you see Letterman last night?"

Mr. H is allowing students to correct their own homework, "You're on your own; you're doing your own cheating."

Although he started the class angry with him, Mr. H makes two trips to Jeff's desk to try to work out scheduling the test and lab.

Teacher: I'd let you do the lab now but I have a filmstrip coming up. It'll be review for everyone but you. When can you come in and do the lab?
Jeff: How long will it take?
Teacher: Fifteen minutes.
Jeff: My lunch hour!
Teacher: Okay.

Mr. H puts off the lights and Dan, with his leg in a cast, tries to move to get a better view.

Teacher: Can't you see Dan? Forget your glasses again? Wanna use mine? (takes off his glasses and hands them to the student, who accepts them.) Why don't you move over there so you can see? I hate to see you strain those muscles.

Football player Dan leaves his crutches on the floor beside his desk and hops on one leg over to a seat directly in front of the screen.

Teacher (realizes that his leg is in a cast): Whoops, another weak muscle.

Later Mr. H tells me Dan has lost so many contact lenses that his parents refuse to buy him any more new ones. After the filmstrip the class is allowed to work quietly and use up the last ten minutes of the class any way they want.

On the board is written: "Review question '. . . in a titration 27.4 milliliters are the standard solution of 0.0154 milliliters. BA (OH) 2 is added to 20.0 milliliters sample of an HCL solution. What is the molarity of the acid? Question 4, What is the molarity of the acid in No. 3 if the acid is H2SO4?'" But the review question holds little interest for Jeff, more buddy than budding chemist:

Jeff (speaking in a low voice): Where were you on Tuesday? You didn't come over.
Neighbor: I was busy
Jeff (sarcastically): I-was-busy. It was my birthday! I haven't had a real birthday since I was 12! Why didn't you come?
Neighbor mumbles something.
Jeff (disgusted): Pissy dickhead.

Student directly in front of me waits until the teacher has turned to the board, grabs the squeeze bottle of soapy water from the lab counter and starts hitting everybody in the back of the head with a stream of water. It's the perfect trick, silent but deadly. One boy whispers, Hey, you bastard! The perpetrator, doubling his duplicity, motions with his thumb passing his ear that I did it. I shake my head to the victims. For a moment we're all in this together. Everyone but the teacher has seen the class clown's transient satisfaction at getting away with something in a strict classroom.

This class demonstrates the difference between a drive and a value. The drive is all from the teacher's end of the room. He wants everyone to know that Jeff is a rule-breaker and that he is impatient with him. The class does not hear the effort he makes for Jeff to make up work, which actually exemplifies the value of respect for the individual, for Jeff's need to do the lab before the test. Mr. H does this arranging one on one. The teacher's drive is for completion of requirements and punctual test taking. The value (the humane thought) is for personal consideration and friendship. The first is public, loud, teacher to rule-breaker ("*You have nothing?*") The second is private, quiet, teacher to rule-breaker ("*I'd let you do it now but I have a filmstrip.*") and inevitably, rule-breaker to pal (*"It was my birthday!"*) These drives and values live side by side in the same space for fifty-five minutes, the "value," Henry tells us, acting as a brake on the "drive." But why is the drive the publicly learned lesson, and the value the privately inculcated attribute? Maybe because what is expected in public schooling is that they will teach rules, not teach forgiveness when they are broken.

Jeff will remember this accommodation from a teacher a little longer than the lab: the unexpected act of kindness resonates in one's memory for a while. So for Jeff, Mr. H's assistance will mitigate the tendency to act as if the teacher were the enemy. The other as-if, to act like the lessons are the important part of school, seems to be the modus operandi of everybody there. A high school class has a formal aspect, recognizable from coast to coast, in city and farm town: a teacher and a large group of young people ostensibly accomplishing a shared educational agenda. I came to see that beyond the formal aspect, there is an underlying, informal but equally powerful "agenda," which excludes the teacher. (One student described a trick they played on the teacher by reversing all the furniture in the room one day in the last week of school; that is an example of the informal agenda finally breaking out of its invisible boundaries to include the teacher.) On the informal agenda, more fluid than its formal counterpart, someone is ever ready to activate a modest illicit plan, pass a peacemaking note, or make a surreptitious joke: the squirt bottle trick bursts through the air, a relief from the tedium of the review (*"In a titration 27.4 milliliters . . ."*) Like rows of little plants, the class is briefly revivified by the water. It's over in a few seconds but it served its purpose: kids are annoyed, amused, amazed that he got away with it. But no one speaks of the soaking; the unaware teacher and all others carry on, acting as if the lesson were the important thing.

Acting as if all in class are seriously on-task, committed to learning, is a trans-generational school "as-if." Obviously, the common good of the mammoth enterprise called public education requires, first, a certain orderliness. Getting twenty-five different personalities (times dozens and dozens of classrooms in a building) to put aside their preoccupations (love, work, weight, the game, the call, the car) and switch gears (topic, teacher, rules, tests) every fifty-five minutes, hour after hour, demands a lot of attention to mutual expectations. And, first among them, is a polite orderliness. Unfortunately, a lot of teaching seems to be more about *creating order* than learning seems to be about *creative thinking*. (Some educators might even think the two goals are incompatible.) I would like to suggest that teachers "drill on," "yell at," and "freak out about" students, not so much because they regret students' failure to apply themselves (*"I'm not going to beg for workbooks"*) but more likely because orderliness is paramount in schools. When students act up or shut down it is a violation of the pretense, shared by everyone, teacher and student, that kids are interested in the molarities of acids, say, or solving for "a." The teacher has not created a vivid presence in their imaginations for her subject (*"School is tedious"*) but all parties in these quiet schools operate politely as if she has. They do so because school cannot grind on in safe, predictable fashion if people start pointing out that all the adults' efforts are of minimal consequence to the students. Schools cannot grind on in an orderly fashion (a "drive") if everybody acts on the fact that, for students, their group's "friendly intimacy"[18] (a "value") counts more than the curriculum. In short, orderliness demands allegiance from all, to the "Lessons-Are-The-Important-Part-Of-School" *as-if.*

NOTES

1. Whitehead, Alfred North (1929/1967), *The Aims of Education and Other Essays*, NY: Free Press, p.1.

2. Henry, Jules (1963), *Culture Against Man*, NY: Vintage, p.14.

3. Romine, Stephan A. (1954), *Building the High School Curriculum,* NY: The Ronald Press, p.28.

4. One North Dakota high school with an enrollment of 900 students listed 222 courses in its 1998 catalogue.

5. Dorris, Michael (1987), *Yellow Raft, Blue Water*, NY: H. Holt.

6. Henry, Jules (1963), *Culture Against Man*, NY: Vintage Books, p.361.

7. "I found there a firmly entrenched pattern of pupil hostility toward the teacher and toward nearly every nonmaterial aspect of the way of life the teacher represented . . . In a setting in which critical differences between a teacher and his pupils are rooted in antagonisms of cultural rather than classroom origins, I believe that the teacher might succeed in coping more effectively with conflict and in capitalizing on his instructional efforts if he were to recognize and to analyze his ascribed role as 'enemy' rather than attempt to ignore or to deny it," in Spindler, George D. (1974), "The Teacher as Enemy," in *Education and the Cultural Process: Toward an Anthropology of Education,* (2nd ed.), NY: Holt, Rinehart, p.77.

8. Russell, Bertrand (1951), *The Autobiography of Bertrand Russell*, Boston: Little, Brown, p.191.

9. Whitehead, Alfred North and Bertrand Russell (1912/1927), *Principia Mathematica*, Cambridge, England: University Press.

10. The mimetic style of teaching is one in which there is a transmission of factual and procedural knowledge from one person to another; the student imitates the teacher. The transformative style is one in which there is a qualitative change in the pupil as a result of the teaching. See: Jackson, Philip (1986), *The Practice of Teaching*, NY: Teachers College, p.129.

11. Criterion-referenced evaluations are meant to illustrate a student's mastery of the material; norm-referenced evaluations compare a student's performance to that of a normative group. See: McNeil, John D. (1977), *Curriculum: A Comprehensive Introduction*, Boston: Little Brown, pp.146.

12. "The Burnouts develop a culture that is dominated by the private and opposed to the institutional . . . [they] attend school because it is necessary, but focus their attention on relations and activities whose locus is independent from the school," in: Eckert, Penelope (1989), *Jocks and Burnouts: Social Categories and Identity in the High School*, NY: Teachers College Press, p.103.

13. "In all, over half the students (52%) could think of nothing related to the school curriculum that gave them a sense of accomplishment. Rather, what sense of accomplishment they did earn in school came from sports and other extracurricular activities (20%), socializing with friends (11%) or . . . nothing at all (21%)," in, Shaw, Robert A. 1982) unpublished paper, Brown University; cited in Sizer, Theodore (1985), *Horace's Compromise: The Dilemma of the American High School,* Boston: Houghton Mifflen, p.56.

14. Whitehead, Alfred North (1938/1966), *Modes of Thought*, NY: Macmillan, p.138.

15. Schlegel, Alice and Herbert Barry III (1991), *Adolescence: An Anthropological Inquiry*, NY: The Free Press, p.26.

16. North Dakota Youth Risk Behavior Survey, North Dakota Department of Public Instruction, 1997.

17. U.S. Office of Education, Reports on Class Size, Smaller Learning Environments," in *Turning Points: Preparing American Youth for the 21st Century* (1990), NY: Carnegie Council on Adolescent Development.

18. Henry, Jules (1963), *Culture Against Man,* NY: Vintage Books, p.14.

Chapter Six

Engaging the Disengaged

"I felt like, well, this is a lot of education I'm getting in this class period, but I do not really know if I'm learning it or not."

Melanie, Grade 11

***

"Education is the acquisition of the art of living."

Alfred North Whitehead[1]

Melanie's dilemma is not unusual. She thinks that the education she is "getting" (and regarding it as something she receives instead of works on is the problem) from the adults in her school is not something she can remember. By now she has acquired the "art of living" *in* school but it has been by her wits, that is, her ability to nimbly negotiate her relationships. Melanie sees the dichotomy between what is intended in the curriculum and what she takes away from school. She's not sure she's learning it? Of course she isn't, not if learning means considering it, reflecting on the evidence for it, imagining different perspectives towards it, ruminating about its implications, recognizing its connections to other knowledge she is constructing, feeling its relevance to various aspects of her seventeen-year-old existence. (Would Melanie even regard these as legitimate modes of thought?) Melanie is not learning it, if learning means engaging with it. I met many students who were enjoying school, especially their favorite subject(s) and extracurricular activities, but who, by the end of their junior year, said they were getting a little nervous. They did not feel prepared to graduate because they attended school life more studiously than they attended to school subjects.[2] And those are two very separate entities, as the conversations in the preceding chapters indicate. It was as though they had been on a train ride and had spent their time chatting-up the other passengers instead of mastering the schedule with the conductor (and besides, the conductor is the enemy). Melanie is worried that the train is pulling into the last station—her senior year—and she hasn't learned her education yet. She has not been engaged in a meaningful way for the past several years. She doesn't say that meaninglessness is the problem; she just thinks that by being lazy in her homework, distracted in her classes and taught by people who seem mostly interested in testing her every five minutes (when they aren't playing favorites) she fears she is failing. Imagine her dread of the hard-duty memorizing she thinks she has to do, to learn all of *it* for the college boards coming up.

Melanie is impressed by the sheer size and efficiency (*"a lot of education . . . in this period"*) of the whole enterprise. And like most of her peers, she is loyal to her school and proud of its public profile. But she does not know what she has retained, so she is insecure. Throughout her high school years she has felt her way through an exhausting list of emotions, ranging anywhere from anxious to zombie-like. These emotions are not experienced by all students every day, but probably by most at one time or another, in ways that would surprise adults in the same setting. One student told me rather sadly, "School's not what people think it is, you know." What school is, frequently, is feeling coerced to learn what the teacher wants them to learn; feeling bothered a lot of the time (bored by many subjects; angry at each other for being "snots;" stressed out by teacher indifference to their crowded lives; and feeling bewildered at new material taught by teachers who can seem unconcerned whether they understand it or not. These emotions may not be universally experienced, but they are universally recognizable by the students—which makes them members of the same culture,[3] or sub-culture.

Members of a culture obey its formal, explicit rules (getting vaccinated, registering to vote, applying for a marriage license). They also will have informal rules, or customs, which, though not strictly followed by all, have implications understood by all (attending a Fourth of July parade, standing for the "Star Spangled Banner," eating a hot dog at a ballgame). A culture's explicit rules, for example, classes will begin at 8:00, actually are posted somewhere. And infraction of explicit rules receives explicit punishment, for example, 3 tardies gets a detention. Implicit rules, for example, newcomers to the school will sit in one section of the lunchroom, are communicated only symbolically. And infraction of implicit rules receives implicit punishment, so a sophomore who sits with juniors at lunch will be ignored. One thing that makes a teen group a cohesive subculture is the fact that the punishment for implicit rule infraction hurts their feelings more than the punishment for explicit rule infraction (everyone claimed they would prefer being dropped from class because of a failing grade to dressing differently). We recall Jeff (Chapter 5) who was more hurt by his friend forgetting his birthday than he was by the teacher's demand to see him after class. This is because following explicit rules, like stopping at a red light, are basically affect*less* actions for the person, while choosing to follow implicit rules has an emotional component, just out of our awareness. I think observing customs circumscribes our lives with a certain satisfying predictability. Not observing a custom might make us feel vaguely guilty; seeing a custom go unobserved by a person we understood to be a co-member of our culture feels like a letdown. The rhythms of our customs comfort because they help us to make sense in a chaotic world. We might not be aware of just how used we are to eating turkey on Thanksgiving until someone suggests a tuna sandwich in its place; or how much we count on the weekly call to a distant parent until the time comes when we can't make it anymore.

A culture's member recognizes (from the Latin, "knows again") a co-member because of the constellation of shared implicit rules around which, and through which, they communicate. The secondary school teen subculture[4] is identifiable by its broad, unwritten guidelines about dialect, dress, fun, food, music, social obligations, study habits, leisure habits, employment choices, cheating tendencies, drinking customs, mating rituals, and authority hierarchies. All of these things give the subculture a loose coherence, more or less edifying to its members and mystifying to nonmembers. Under their big umbrella of customs, teens typically tolerate differences, so one student might swear like a trooper and another just precede every verb or noun with the word "like;" one could come to school as a Hippy Wanna-Be (*"blue crappy clothing"*) and another like a Headbanger (*"black crappy clothing"*); one might like listening to heavy metal and another like singing gospel; one might have had two terminated pregnancies and another have taken a vow of abstinence. Adopting just one aspect of appearance or habit does not make the teen a subculture member; it is several styles and habits, taken together, which make him recognizable (comprehensible) to his peers. Teens would allow, I expect, virtually all variations on the adolescent theme except imitation of the adult "group." The appearance in the cafeteria of a boy their age, in a suit and tie, marveling at the macaroni and cheese and explaining the merits of Wayne Newton's voice would be absolutely guaranteed to be shunned by every clique, isolated faster than you could say white-shoes-and-belt. In short, the distinguishing characteristic of the teen subculture is that they are Not The Adults. They must act, speak, dress and believe differently from *them*. Proof for this would be the fact that students from any of the schools I visited could drop out of one school and join another (and they do), hardly be noticed, and eventually feel as though they fit right in. If an adult tried to join them (and I did), by sitting among them in class, at lunch or the game, she would be the object of some curiosity. Eventually kids get used to an adult in their midst; they'll be friendly, even in their own way, welcoming. But they won't invite her to watch and listen to their sacred ritual (their conversations) because it would change the ritual too drastically. (Long conversations with teens, on their turf, have to be by pre-arrangement, and then it is a conversation the adult is essentially guiding.)

Their subculture shapes—in varying degrees according to the individual—students' perceptions of school every bit as powerfully as the environment shapes Eskimos' perceptions of many types of snow. After listening to these students for months I would say that the subculture virtually overpowers the school's curriculum, that is to say it captures students' attention and allegiance. For one thing, the curriculum at least stops occasionally: teachers give the period over to a study hall, a guest speaker causes an impromptu school assembly, a snowstorm cancels classes. And school does end for most at 3:30. But the subculture never, ever lets down; it actually gears up in all those moments when the curriculum relaxes. The worldview that they are not the adults accompanies them to work, at home and on all their encounters with each other. It is reified in dozens of conversations all day long. Their subculture is as complicated as the 200-item school curriculum—in fact, I think it is more complicated because it is rule-driven, yet the rules are re-negotiated silently by all the participants. For example, the "rule" that you consider a class boring when the teacher requires silent attention to his teaching is broken by students who appreciate a demanding teacher's personal interest in their progress. English teacher Mrs. E (chapter 2), biology teacher Mr. M (chapter 5), Spanish teacher Mr. A (chapter 5) and chemistry teacher Mr. H (chapter 5) are all "great" that is to say, their classes are exceptions to this rule. The rule that teachers' pets are despised and yet, overlooking "a certain amount of brownnosing" is another. The rule that cliques are mutually exclusive and yet a Prep (*"always dresses up for school"*) and a Grunge (*"they just look cruddy"*) getting along well (*"I'm kinda rounded out in my friends"*) is yet another. Subtly and continuously redeveloping and relearning rules within the teen subculture is a more intense school experience than learning any piece of curriculum we could design. I think those of us interested in school improvement ignore that fact at our peril.

The bitter contrast between what educators intend to happen in schools (the teaching and curriculum) and how kids feel about what happens in schools (defined by their subculture) is demonstrated in Melanie's plaintive statement (*"not sure if I'm really learning it or not."*) The adults are busily "giving" a lot of education and the adolescents are not so busily "getting" it. The fit of adult-developed curriculum and adolescent preoccupations is always uncomfortable, a perennial problem as old as schooling itself. The difference between their respective activities is obviously one of responsibility and role. Despite, or because of these differences, progressive educators work hard at making the coursework relevant to students' lives. I am convinced, however, that updating the subjects for study is not the answer to student alienation. In fact, kids are not alienated from these schools; most of them like to be in these schools (*"I like school, you know? That's where I go to find out what's going on!"*) They are alienated, however, from the teaching: how the curriculum is constructed. Educators know something isn't working (they listen to their own children at home, if nothing else) and spend countless hours and dollars designing a more modern list of subjects. Some of these innovations work well (computer science courses are now so routine in schools that students graduate with a sophistication their parents will accomplish only with concentrated study). Nevertheless, I found that students generally are as resistant to being taught as they ever were. Their subculture reinforces the attitude that, "school is a drag" because of the perception that teachers are mildly-to-extremely coercive, boring or neglectful.

I would suggest that attempts to improve schooling go in the wrong direction. Rather than continually adding new subjects to old, I think we need to consider the learners and how we can engage them more effectively. To do this we need to reassess a closely held, and broadly operational, belief: that teachers deliver knowledge that students receive, that teachers talk and (as a consequence) students *know*.

THE REQUIREMENT OF RECALL

"I can do it and get a good grade. I won't remember it though."

Richard, Grade 11

***

"An articulated memory is the gift of language, considered as an expression from oneself in the past to oneself in the present."

Alfred North Whitehead[5]

Like most people, teachers typically regard knowledge is a thing that exists outside, and independent of the learner. As such, it can be transmitted with serious intent, if not ease, from one person to another. Effective teaching then becomes reduced to clarity, sequence and organization. These are admirable attributes, ones that we count on in a good slide show. For good teaching they might even be necessary; but they surely are not sufficient. If knowledge is a transferable thing, then the teacher becomes a type of archeologist, who earnestly goes on ahead, discovers an (arti)fact, catalogues it and passes it down to the next generation, the youngsters scaling the academic heights below him. One's education is then an ever-lengthening list of artifacts to acquire, nuggets to store in a "mental backpack." But this learning is necessarily superficial and, in terms of its process, depressingly and ennervatingly repetitious: acquired and tested-for, acquired and tested-for, acquired and tested-for. Furthermore it is anxiety-producing for the student because he believes he has to expand that mental backpack almost infinitely (*"[Teachers] are always trying to pack it in and there's not enough room!"*) The mechanistic metaphors students used to describe their own learning were jarring to hear. They conveyed the notion of learning as work they had to force themselves to do, in order to add to the stuff in the container they called their mind. This attitude of student-mind-as-container (we'll call it Tupperware Teaching) is one that is acquired *in* school. They surely do not have it when they first arrive. By the time they get to school, young children have already acquired a complex language that crisscrosses itself with tenses, pronouns, modifiers, qualifiers, subject-verb agreements and non-verbal symbols (the vocabulary by age 5 averages an impressive 2,000 words,[6] but that's really the least of it). They have acquired this sophisticated mode of communicating, as well as a sizable repertoire of socially appropriate behavior, unselfconsciously, almost organically. This, the most important learning of their lives, has been accomplished before they ever walk into a school, without any adult implying: I am teaching you something now, using a language slightly different from the one you use with people you know well, and afterwards you will show me that you remember it by using a pencil and paper. It is this new accountability that shapes so powerfully students' earliest understandings of how they themselves learn. They come to see themselves at a very young age as *pupils,* who must now show strangers that they know what they intend for them to know.[7] Before very many years have passed, schools teach students that they learn by hard study. And they do learn by hard study! But that is just a part of the picture. Students also learn through their senses, by having their imaginations stimulated, by having their emotions involved, and making meaning in thousands and thousands of dialogues.[8] Creswell writes:

> Knowledge is within the meanings people make of it; knowledge is gained through people *talking about their meanings*; knowledge is laced with personal biases and values; knowledge is written in a personal, up-close way; and knowledge evolves, emerges, and is inextricably tied to the context in which it is studied.[9] (emphasis added)

Knowledge studied in schools is inextricably tied to the testing context. This *requirement of recall* satisfies—not the young student, who has a natural, easy, irresistible inclination to learn—but the adults, who must demonstrate to others that learning has occurred, especially as measured against others of like age. That is all well and good except that the student begins to believe that his own learning is significant, not when it is meaningful to him, but when it is *demonstrable* to others. Eventually, trying to learn just that which is demonstrable becomes the compulsive course of action for students (when in fact they do choose to act in their student role). If only they would (could!) put the amount of energy into reading, writing, reflecting, experimenting, creating and evolving (to use Creswell's word) their own knowledge, that they put into cramming for the test on Friday, or worrying about "pop quizzes." By the time they get to be high school juniors, they will define their learning in completely operational terms: they know something if they are able to specifically recall and note it. Furthermore, they will come to believe that courses in which "truth" is negotiable, that is, where the teacher encourages students' own ideas, are courses with a lower standard of excellence: since nobody knows, anything goes! (And we saw in Chapter 2 that if students believe that, despite open class discussion, the testing still requires the teacher's answers, they will develop a cynicism about the whole genre of the humanities.) By the time they are eighteen, after twelve years of habitual disengagement and test taking, students will arrive at college preferring classes that require only listening and note-taking skills. These are the skills needed for what we have called elsewhere technical knowing,[10] that is to say, publicly transferable information. It will then take some convincing for a professor to make them see that their own interpretations and questions are not only valid, they are required for everybody's growth, even (or especially) the professor's. In his landmark book on mind and ideas, Gregory Bateson describes a class he taught to psychiatric residents, presumably mature people who had already succeeded at twelve years of schooling and eight years of higher education. His comments illustrate the difference between the notion of learning as publicly transferable knowledge and learning as an internal, evolving process of construction:

> [The residents] would attend dutifully and even with intense interest to what I was saying, but every year the question would arise after three or four sessions of the class: What is this course all about? . . . Gradually I discovered that what made it difficult to tell the class what the course was about was the fact that my way of thinking was different from theirs. A clue to this difference came from one of the students. It was the first session of the class and I had talked about the cultural differences between England and America—a matter which should always be touched on when an Englishman must teach Americans about cultural anthropology. At the end of the session, one resident came up. He glanced over his shoulder to be sure the others were all leaving, and then said rather hesitantly, "I

want to ask you a question." "Yes." "It's—do you want us to learn what you are telling us? Or is it all a sort of example, an illustration of something else?" "Yes, indeed!"[11]

As it happens, a medical student is no more sophisticated in this matter than our seventeen year-old Melanie: she too believes she is supposed to learn exactly what teachers speak to her, instead of developing her ability to see interconnections among knowledge, to weigh evidence, to seek alternative explanations. Whitehead once complained, "The great English universities, under whose direct authority school children are examined in plays of Shakespeare, to the certain destruction of their enjoyment, should be prosecuted for soul murder."[12] Or: many teachers want students to learn what they are being told (to be "examined" later) instead of (enjoying) interpreting it.

By converting early the experience of coming to know into a learning activity that satisfies an adult's requirement of recall, schools have managed to reduce the miracle that separates the human from the rest of nature (because we know that we know) into an increasingly boring task. The "soul is murdered," that is, the student comes to see that linearity and reductionistic thinking (some would say, a certain simple-mindedness) are rewarded, and that his mind's natural intuitiveness and free-ranging curiosity (some would say, a certain muddle-headedness) are not rewarded. Surely both modes of knowing, linear and intuitive, are desirable and appropriate; they complement each other well in various situations.[13] But the secondary schools test for one and tend to ignore, or dispatch to after-school activities, the other. Technical knowledge is necessary for successful functioning in a society, we would all agree. Those times tables, for example, are as durable as old radiators. And by requiring the study of technical knowledge, teachers are accomplishing another goal, that of having teenagers learn a valuable self-discipline. (The popular taskmaster Mr. M (Chapter 5) of biology fame, demanded straight-out memorization of bird slides, nevertheless he had crowds of students in his courses. They basked in his devotion to their success, which dovetailed with his formidable commitment to science.)

Significant knowing may include technical knowing, but it also has meaning for the learner, that is to say, it is apprehended in terms of its importance to her (learning how to drive a car is pretty technical, but it is about as significant a piece of learning for a teenager as we can envision). "Importance"[14] here refers not to its usefulness but to the value it has to her past, present and future life, a more complicated epistemological notion than mere utility. Significant knowing may also happen through an intuitive appreciation of music, metaphor, poetry, drama, liturgy, dreams or even mystical experience. It is remembered because it is, for want of a better word, felt,[15] that is, *connected* in a diffuse way to the student's unique repertoire of experiences, intellectual, emotional and physical. This imaginative connection then gives rise to a change in the way she views her past and anticipates her future. Significant knowing can also be accomplished through our senses, a mode more familiar to the artist or liturgical participant. King notes the difference:

> I remember an art major friend at Iowa who reported a moment in a course in which the professor was describing some kind of festival in China or Japan—a huge revelry, fully described, in which one of the celebrations was to throw packets of colored powders in each other's faces! My friend was struck by this activity and sat, stunned, imagining it in all its violence and color and festivity. Coming out of his "mind-blown" state, he looked around—all the students were bending over their notebooks dutifully inscribing, "They throw packets of colored powder at each other," in their notes. This was, presumably, without the actual activity, the feel and sense of it, having passed through their consciousness. Those moments must be 'felt' to be 'learned' in any but the most limited sense of the word 'learned.'[16]

Knowledge about this revelry will be limited, unless accompanied by time to pose provocative questions that involve the students in a full discussion. The problem in schools is that with every passing year, the curriculum's "packets of colored powder" become inexorably things that students read and hear *about* instead of experience. (At what point does school become boring? Could it be as early as Grade 4? 5? And it often stays that way for ten long years, until you might choose your college major, that is, something that excites your imagination.) What is the solution? We can't start making the school experience a totally artistic or religious experience and expect to keep our jobs very long. What we need is an approach to teaching that will require more participation[17] from everyone, one that will require discovery and ideally, application, of knowledge ("*I think you learn more when you know how it applies to you! And you're willing to learn more . . . and it stays with you too*"). Whitehead said get your knowledge early and use it. I am suggesting that this sound advice is problematic because the teen subculture has an unwritten rule against engaging wholeheartedly in the school's entire formal system, a system whose talisman is the course schedule and whose delegated representative is the enemy/teacher.

Educational philosophers from Rousseau[18] to Whitehead[19] to Dewey[20] have pointed out that first-hand knowledge is the ultimate basis of an intellectual life. Perhaps it is worthy of note that these eminent thinkers were country-raised: Rousseau in France, Whitehead in England and Dewey in Vermont. They were wide-awake, to use Maxine Greene's[21] great term, to their vividly instructive rural childhoods. Rousseau particularly, saw school as a distraction from learning; he had the fictitious Emil and his tutor avoid the corrupting influences of the schoolhouse until he was well into adolescence. Dewey insisted that school be connected to, not abstracted from life. Whitehead himself never saw the inside of a classroom until he was fourteen; as an adult, he would disparage those who "could know all about the atmosphere and miss the radiance of the sunset."[22] A hundred years later Walker Percy takes up the alarm on behalf of the secondary student:

> A student who has the desire to get at a dogfish or a Shakespeare sonnet may have the greatest difficulty in salvaging the creature itself from the educational package in which it is presented. The new textbook, the type, the smell of the page, the classroom, the aluminum windows and the winter sky, the personality of Miss Hawkins—these media which are supposed to transmit the sonnet may only succeed in transmitting themselves. It is only the hardiest and cleverest of students who can salvage the sonnet from this many-tissued package. It is only the rarest student who knows the sonnet must be salvaged from the package.[23]

Constructing her own new appreciation of the dogfish or the sonnet is difficult because of what I would call the "cellophane of schooling." The object of study is typically twice removed from the modern student. First, the object is not available in its own context: the dogfish is out of water, pins holding it firmly to the dissection board; the sonnet is in the middle of a fat anthology, wedged between Chaucer and Tennyson. The possibility of naively encountering the fish or sonnet, and exploring their properties out of the student's own need to understand ("discovery learning") is constrained by budget and time. In the second displacement, the "shrink-wrapped" subject comes to be understood only in terms of an expert's theory. What others have said is what the student knows about it; she learns what others have discovered *for* her.

Where they "succeed," the schools make the familiar strange. They have to do that to make the private individual a member of a larger community. Ideally her education helps a student take her experience and place it in a broader context so it can be compared, contrasted and built upon. Unfortunately schools do a really good job of it, going swiftly from the concrete to the general, raising the study of "X" to such a level of abstraction that the subject itself is radically devalued. After about ten years in school the student perceives the subjects of the curriculum as *less real,* and the theories the experts have evolved about them more real. Life is reduced to a mere exemplification of someone's interpretation. I see this as a loss, and a double one at that. First, having lost sovereignty over her own interpretation (because she relies on the teacher and textbook author to tell her), the student doesn't even miss it; she judges her success at knowing only in terms of how closely she approximates the experts' versions. And second, she has lost any assurance that what she discovers would have value not only for herself but possibly for her class-mates and teachers. A certain amount of "cellophane-wrap" of school subject is absolutely inevitable. Our millions of secondary students will never have a real encounter with a dogfish (and Romantic Rousseau *is* dead these 200 years). What is objectionable is sanctifying the cellophane wrap to the neg-lect of the student.

REMEDIATIONS

"This is what I do: I work on staying together, one day at a time. There's no room for anything else. It takes all my energy."

Bobbie Ann Mason[24]

***

"Our interpretations of experience determine the limits of what we can do in the world."

Alfred North Whitehead[25]

How is a curriculum not like a hockey game? It is not like a hockey game be-cause it is not about sending in a fresh line when the old one slows down. A complete revision of the curriculum in terms of modernity's issues (every-thing from computer-assisted drafting to childcare) does not help if the old concept of instruction-as-information-delivery endures. The modern philoso-pher Robert Brumbaugh has written, "Pragmatically, it is surprising how such minor modifications as movable furniture and some tolerance for student ac-tion improve the situation [in school]."[26] Moving the desks and tolerating some student action might improve the situation a bit, but to the extent that these things pass for genuine structural reforms based on a mutual commit-ment of all parties, such modifications are not merely minor, they are a little risky. They might lull teachers, who believe that the New Age has blessedly arrived in their classrooms, into a political passivity. Human interaction in a social space—a natural enough phenomenon—is seen by some rock-ribbed traditionalists as incompatible with "true" learning (because scholarly study is done in isolation, or at least silently). However most teachers tolerate it to a degree today as a means of, 1.) demonstrating that they have moved beyond the nineteenth century in their pedagogy and, 2.) guaranteeing that students will respond more positively to the learning environment (*"If I could not see and talk to my friends during and between classes? I would go nutmeg! And lose my mind"*).[27] Small group work and cooperative learning have become the open classroom movement of the nineties. I saw many instances of it every day but often it was not organized thoughtfully (*"Have your desks anyway. I don't care"*). so that groups quickly got off task. How does a student teacher expect kids to help each other on a math problem when they have to read each other's work upside down? This is an example of a good solution (group work) which actually makes the "problem" (learning math) worse, because the students may end up not taking the subject itself seriously. They look around, see that people in other groups look, shall we say, unfascinated by the material, and give it up themselves. And, ever ready, the informal subculture kicks right in. These days, if teachers tried to eliminate small group work from their pedagogy they would meet resistance. The students enjoy it (*"Being with friends helps to get the jitterness out"*). Truth to tell, the teacher hopes that, for a few minutes anyway, the smart kids will translate the content, using their own inimitable colloquialisms, to the not-as-smart kids. And everybody will learn cooperation. It works on so many levels, it seems too good to be true.

Maybe it is. As reforms go, group learning reminds me of Falk's "Disneyland Postmodernism,"[28] his term to describe the New Age movements that promise salvation without any transitional unpleasantness. Group learning is postmodern*istic* in that it rejects competition within the classroom, but at best it is really just a transitional pleasantness (students get to talk to each other—the real benefit, to them, of going to school), because if, while a teacher employs group learning in her class, the cultural glue of her institution as a whole is still coercion, the result is most regrettable: students receive the double message that "you should cooperate if you're young, but you grow out of the need for it." And if receiving double messages does not produce schizophrenics, as Bateson[29] predicts, at the very least it will produce cynics, the toughest crowd to educate. I wonder, when the old hierarchy of principal-teacher-student still obtains in all "important" matters (rules, schedules, content, grades, resources), where is the vision of cooperation that will inspire imitation? "Do as I say, not as I do" is still an unfailing recipe for raising confused and ultimately disrespectful children.

And as far as a theory of knowing is concerned, moving the furniture does not change the fundamental idea in most educators' minds that the student and teacher are separate from each other and separate from the material. What Brumbaugh calls the school's "insulating space"—which makes disaffected students feel completely unconnected to each other—still separates all the parties. Knowledge is still presumed to be something like an isolated beep on a wireless sent out by the teacher and received, intact and identically, by 25 different sets (we'll call it the Marconi Epistemology). The idea that the message is received instead by 25 different and dynamic little Marconis, each with an urge to reshape it, that is to say, connect it to his own experience, is not taken into account. Not only that, even when the "wireless" is manned by a cooperating group of four, the known, Percy would say, still has sovereignty over the knowers.[30]

My suggestion to insure that the student's unique way of reconstructing knowledge new to him is fundamentally respected, is first of all, to provide the student with new experience or information (remember the information is not knowledge; it becomes knowledge with interpretation) and then have a genuine dialogue about it. The first great teacher of recorded history, Socrates, taught us to teach this way. Some might say this suggestion just reinvents the wheel, that group work takes care of this need for students to speak to each other about what they are learning. But what I am suggesting is slightly different. I think that the group that cooperates has to get bigger and the class, as a whole must get smaller.[31] This would have salutary effects educationally and socially. In effect, the class becomes the cooperating group, and the teacher takes a much more interactive role.[32] Instead of a class of 24, with six cooperating groups of four each, or more typically, a class of 24 with one teacher talking, 8 kids listening, and 12 kids up to something else, I am suggesting a class, numbering around 12 to 15, which *works together*. The dialogue, guided by the teacher, is one that everyone, per force, hears. And takes part in. The form of the class, that is, its size and physical arrangement, changes; as a result the function of the class is enhanced. Insulating spaces would tend to disappear. As well, the philosophically impoverished notion that the teacher sends out knowledge, which is then received wholesale by students would begin to change.

Addressing a large problem (student disengagement) with a simple-sounding solution (small seminars) is not unlike the "broken window theory"[33] of urban decay. According to its authors, if a broken window in a building is left unrepaired, it is a signal that no one cares. Before long all the rest of the windows get broken too. The research suggests that "small, untended behaviors" lead to a broad breakdown of community controls, that is, urban decay. Fix the first broken windows and the community tends to stay (socially) healthy. I believe that in classes as large as 20 to 25, secondary students seize the opportunity to engage in many small behaviors that go untended by the teacher. These behaviors include writing other homework, reading other material, gossiping, flirting, note-writing, hair-combing, make-up applying and removing, sleeping,[34] daydreaming, stressing-out, clowning around, cheating, and invariably, conversations, "sotto voce," with seatmates about everything under the sun except the class topic. We do not need a very high percentage of the class doing these things to have a generalized disengagement, a dissipation of energy, a breakdown of a genuine dialogue about the subject (*"It's so hard to speak in front of people who don't care about being there."*) A true conversation never takes hold, as overworked teachers teach to the interested students, and resort to a dispiriting, coercive style with the uninterested students. Such bifurcation of practice leads in time to teacher burnout ("*In 8th grade we caused a science teacher to resign . . . I'm not that much of a troublemaker but, egged on, I can go rather far*"), a disaster that might well be avoided if only teacher and students sat face to face, really looking at and listening to each other. It's hard to be inattentive, let alone rude, in a circle of a dozen people. It's hard to get exasperated by student indifference if you see every face and hear every voice. In only one class in three schools did I see desks drawn into two concentric circles, everyone facing everyone else. (I should note that the poorly performing students (self-identified) did choose to sit in the outer circle, slightly more removed from the teacher. But they all seemed to be engaged in math, albeit with uneven degrees of success.) It was a model-looking math class, taught by a very popular teacher. After he taught a lesson, the students would do exercises or "seat work," and they were completely free to consult their neighbors on either side of them, as long as they were talking about math. One day we came in and the desks were all lined up in the traditional manner because others had used the room for an exam. The students were very upset ("*Why are the desks this way?*"); they quickly moved them into their normal circle and relaxed.

Another consequence of smaller classes is that the evaluation would be more comprehensive yet there would be less of it. But what there is would be more significant. In short there would be more information in the evaluations for the student and parent to consider. Written narratives describing progress, or its absence, would advise those concerned what has to happen for change or development to take place. I believe that it is in the primary grades where we see the best education happening in our schools. It is no coincidence that, in those grades, the first report cards (pre-letter grades) are a true descriptive review of the student's progress. Students seeking the Fine Arts degree receive descriptive reviews of their work. The evaluation includes a letter grade but as well, a description of his development from the place where he began, while taking into account the high ideal of his arts education. Giving an artist a B without advisement as to what she has to do to improve, is an empty mark ("*She's a hard grader but she's not very critical. There's a big difference*"). Why would we think that giving students a grade for scholarship, measured against the progress of *others,* without information tailored toward personal improvement, is any different?

For all of my observational research I sat in the back of classes. The slackers, students-too-busy-to-study, and perpetrators of classroom crime would head back to where I was. The serious students, who loved the subject for itself, or wanted the grade, would stay right under the teacher's nose. Such a class does not coalesce easily into a community, presenting the teacher daily, with a debilitating challenge. Complicating this socio/academic fragmentation was a strong undercurrent I call the student subculture. This subculture complains about, even conspires against, the teaching—to varying extents, depending on the class leadership and the degree of its indifference about learning. This subculture has the invincibility of Old Ironsides: it takes a hit and sails right around (indeed, it thrives on the hits). The subculture does not want the teacher to join them. Its integrity requires that the teacher be different from them in all ways. Teachers should be professional, well educated, older, so the subculture's profile—casual, under-educated, younger—is fortified by the sheer contrast. I do not suggest we attempt a new, all-inclusive, trans-generational coalition of young and old in the classroom. I do not believe the students would respond well to that; they are wary of teachers who try to be their buddies. Students want to participate in just those classes that pique their interest, and they will get by sometimes amazingly well, in the rest. I suggest smaller, seminar-type classes[35] where one adult and 12–14 adolescents sit face to face, and are made accountable to each other for their preparation for, and attention to, the material (note that accountability is not the same as testability); they feel the energy of their joint attention. In short, they have a relationship to the material through each other.[36] In an ideal world they also might find a relationship to each other through the material. My remedy is not new nor is it complicated. It is expensive however, because the increase in the number of teachers is significant. I believe this expense is justified. The current system lets too many students step around the curriculum wearing their big boots of indifference, so it is minimally speaking, a waste of resources. We know from the earliest philosophers that actually participating in one's education is the first step towards accomplishing it. And teachers have every right and responsibility to disallow the many small behaviors that interfere with that participation.

The class's campfire-like form would accomplish a new function, that of engaging students in their own learning. And not incidentally, the teacher is kept more engaged also, putting the issue of the neglectful teacher to rest. Different rules of engagement would mean a more genuine pedagogical relationship too, so the nasty issue of teachers' pets should go away. All the students would be aware of each other and of the teacher because the sheer distance between them would be smaller. This would be a novelty. Their voices would not be strange to one another, their various constructions of knowledge equally considered. They would be less likely to make those inferential leaps about each other based on appearance; the oppression of a social hierarchy based on what they wear might still obtain but its implications for behavior would be attenuated by more knowledge of the other. As proponents of multiculturalism have claimed, the more you understand of a person, the less likely you are to put him or her blindly into a category or class. And eventually, in the give and take of a seminar, students would learn to think on their feet, a skill at least as important as recall. This sort of interaction does happen already everyday in schools, in those places where the relationship between students and the teacher is characterized more by conversation than pedantry. The adult who coaches a team or directs a play or advises the yearbook staff, etc., interacts differently there than he does with those same students in the classroom. After 3:30, the teacher's leadership style, ideally, is strong yet respectful of the students' perspective; the students' participatory style is energetic yet respectful of the teacher's leadership. We would all agree some of the most powerful learning in all of schooling takes places in those after-school venues.[37] (One Ivy League university tells groups of hopeful applicants that about 75% of their college education will take place outside the classroom; this institution invests a substantial percentage of its resources in societies and clubs for that reason.[38]) Students know it too (*"High school will mean nothing to you if you aren't in activities"*). Could it be that after school, the student subculture and the "curriculum" are more integrated? Could it be that in extracurricular activities, the subculture's informal and the school's formal curriculum actually *require*, even reinforce each other? Could it be that the two symbol systems of adults and teens merge in the extra-curriculars, as everyone works to make the collaboration succeed? We recall that the best thing about school, by all reports, is talking to your friends. I would suggest that what happens is, after school, teachers take that pleasantry (communicating with peers), mix it with an activity that has meaning for them (e.g., putting out the newspaper), adopt a more caring stance or at least a more democratic attitude, and convert the whole experience into true teaching moments.[39]

The objections to this recommendation for smaller secondary classes will come from many quarters. The pedant will want to carry on in the *tired* and true manner, doling out pieces of knowledge as if from a treasure box in the attic. Just running a discussion or designing an experience for the students though which they would feel as much as know would take practice for a few. The teacher explores the territory *with* the students, and this is risky. What if they ask questions about connections to other curriculum? Or pose solutions the teacher has not anticipated? I believe secondary teachers who stay enthused through their careers find this is what makes teaching fun and fresh all the time: the unpredictability of much of it, and the new learning that happens for them, the teachers, in the course of teaching. Whitehead told us the in all education, the main cause of failure is staleness.[40] It seems to students as though teachers have confused his diagnosis with a remedy.

Many high school students will not be happy with my solution for their disengagement: They *choose* to be disengaged (*"[My] last paper was a bunch of mullarky! I just lied, along with the kid in front of me"*). Why are we solving a problem that does not exist for them? They are accustomed to participating at will, which usually means those infrequent instances when they are interested, well prepared and rested. The teacher and students in a "campfire configuration" would have to come in willing to take account of each other's presence in the room. That is about as good a place to begin learning as I can imagine. I believe that students will see that being engaged in their own learning (feeling more like apprentices constructing things and less like Tupperware storing things) has an energizing function. And by being connected to each other in a discussion, the chances of understanding another—his point of view *and* his talents, proclivities, the factors that motivate his life—increase. We might all rejoice at a learning environment these days that resulted in students' understanding more about each other.

Finally the taxpayer will howl at the huge expense of hiring new teachers for smaller classes. My answer to that objection is this: As presently constituted, secondary education is actually wasting money because it allows students to opt out of participating, even in excellent schools. Just because we send them to school does not mean that they learn there. We can compel the first, but not the second. What is more, disturbed students can turn into dangerous individuals in a large learning environment that paradoxically does not have room for people to notice alienation. The typical secondary instructional mode disconnects school from society, child from curriculum, and teacher from students. This state of affairs is fraught with academic and social risks to all our children. I would encourage any parent to spend a full day following a child around her high school. Race behind everybody, changing topics and teachers every 55 minutes. Sit in classes that will have a total of 120 or more characters by the end of the day. See if you feel like participating energetically, over and over again. Slouch in the back and listen to the parallel conversations (steel yourself), watch the daydreamers, marvel at the diversity of off-task behavior, keep track of the times the teacher mentions the Test to make them sit up and listen, count the number of times he asks, Any questions? and gets no response. Then decide if this detached existence is a good bargain for your money.

No matter what our college majors, all of us secondary teachers minored in "academic detachment." We learned to be dryly suspect of the emotional, the subjective, the personal. Our college professors, masters at transmitting material, provided fine models. Professors persuade with observable fact, honor the generalizeable, dismiss the particular. Their theories render everyone's personal experience invisible, overlaying it with a dull veneer of unfamiliar language. Not for nothing are large lectures held in echo-y, tiered rooms with scores of listeners at one side and a speaker on the other. The rooms are designed to keep students and their stories at a long arm's length. Such stories would be suffused with feeling, and feeling is un*reason*able. No wonder it is discounted in scientific circles, where they watch, measure and relay the findings to waiting colleagues. Members of higher education aspire to this straightforward, observe-then-share mode of operation. The closest envious professors can come is to boil down the most important information in their subjects, carry it with them into their college halls and set it out, inert, for examination.

In marketing courses, future retailers learn to put as few impediments as possible between the customer and the product: stairs are a bad idea, heavy doors, locked glass cases. You will want the customer to move smoothly on the buying impulse; second steps allow second thoughts. But in college lectures the speaker will often stand behind a podium or a table, or up on a stage; the "customer" thinks twice about approaching, even orally. In any case, the goods, as it were, are delivered. Students sit silently, storing up the information. New teachers emerge from this rarefied atmosphere and find employment in the college's poor relation, the high school. There they earnestly pass on the facts of their major to the next generation of aspiring scholars.[41] And if the aspiring scholars turn out to be high-strung adolescents preoccupied with their relationships, well, their teachers simply stay the course and give themselves good grades, for organization.

But the choice of a mode of teaching is not just limited by a lack of imagination to try something different; high school teachers do hoe a different row. Whereas professors will not make time in the syllabus for student stories or feelings because they have no *place* in the curriculum (the canon crowds them out), teachers cannot make a place in the syllabus for student stories because they have no *time* for them. The pace of the day can be so frantic that teachers need their classrooms to be as predictable, that is, as feeling-free, as possible. Feelings would cause chaos in a social structure built on the shaky legs of restraint.[42] Since the members of these little "societies" change every hour (until the teacher at the end of the day will have taught about 120 students),[43] it is little wonder personal relevancies are not indulged. No indeed, feeling should be for birthdays, football games or flirting. The *last* day of school is about feeling. But not everyday.

Students are not taking full advantage of their education for several reasons: they are tired from their jobs, they are uninterested in a lot of it, they are worried about things they can't talk to their families about. Above all, their subculture says it is definitely not cool to participate in every class. And with all this going on, they have the option to disengage without serious penalty. There are many penalties for rule infraction, ranging from detention to suspension to expulsion, but mere consequences for academic detachment: lower grades. This only impresses the ambitious student who, we know, does not characterize the masses (especially in a state where a high school diploma, not high grades, pretty much qualifies someone for public college acceptance). Furthermore, students can pass the tests without really learning a thing. Woody Allen[44] once said 80% of success is just showing up. These kids don't have to. The teacher and the ambitious kids will do all the classwork, and then everybody studies for the Test (or not) and most will pass. But what do they know? They do learn something of what society needs for them to know in order to *behave* well as citizens, I'll grant the schools that. We have trained them to be punctual and orderly, and to act with courtesy to those different from themselves. This is an impressive accomplishment in a diverse society. But don't we have an obligation to teach them more than orderliness? Don't we have an obligation to teach them to think critically, plan creatively and act empathetically? Accomplishing these goals can make a classroom look messy or sound noisy (and it's tricky to test for) but accomplishing them is more feasible in smaller classes. As in any other situation involving humans in a joint venture, accountability goes up as numbers decrease so the testing issue recedes in importance. And if the classes seem less orderly, well, I agree with Brumbaugh, "School should be inefficient about half the time."[45] We're proud in public education that we've gotten good at efficiency, but efficiency has gotten *us* to the point where students' critical skills, capacity for innovation and empathy for each other are underdeveloped. The classes are so large that only the most committed students participate actively all day long. Average and low-achieving students reported that they feel either too coerced, bothered or bewildered a lot of the time to take advantage of all that school could offer. So they disengage, stay quiet—at least with regard to the curriculum—and spend their energies trying to defeat the system's requirements.

We need to design a learning environment which would encompass the student's version of the "art of living" (Whitehead's aim of education) as well as the community's version of the "art of living." The students' definition would encompass, by their reports, peer dialogue, interaction, fun, humor, trust. How much of a typical learning environment fosters these things? Students tell us friends are a great stress reliever (would educators gain anything by keeping them stressed in class? The answer is yes if their goal is crowd control) so artful living would be learning in classes where they could get to know each other (*"I go to classes where my friends are."*) The community's definition of the art of living would seem to encompass an accountability for what you have learned, respect for the community's traditions, and respect for each other. So we see that education is still essentially a moral enterprise. But the philosopher tells us that moral education requires the habitual vision of greatness, and that might be a lot to ask our teachers to provide on a continual basis. I would suggest two other, more plausible entreaties of educators. First, I think that a good civic education requires the habitual vision of democratic participation (*"I guess if I could change one rule it would be to have more democracy in the school for [us] students."*) And second, a good humanistic education requires the habitual vision of knowledge being individually reconstructed in a respectful atmosphere. I believe participating in a probing "colloquial review" of new knowledge could accomplish both these things.

To substitute the lean agenda of accountability, which requires that a teacher's non-teaching time be kept occupied by clerk and guard duties, with an agenda to help students acquire their education through dialogue and discovery will require other structural changes. Administrators would have to loosen the time constraints that rule students' and teachers' lives; change takes time for reflection as well as action.[46] Teachers need the time and opportunity to communicate with each other. This is a necessary part of the middle school "team teaching" approach but apparently an unaffordable luxury in the departmental organization of most secondary schools, where consulting about students across departments is as rare as in college. As one middle school teacher told me, "At the secondary level, teachers never see each other!" There does have to be time built into the day, or at least time built into the week, where the faculty can get together and talk to one another about correlating their curricula, so students could in turn integrate knowledge more easily. For example, English teachers and history teachers could teach a given epoch at the same time. The benefit of having students in Grade 11 read *Scarlet Letter* while studying Colonial America, *Red Badge of Courage* while studying the Civil War, or *The Great Gatsby* while studying the Roaring Twenties is so commonsensical that I confess I am flabbergasted that it does not happen.[47] Individual teachers do take it upon themselves to do this and they give their students a great gift when they do (*"My English teacher taught something about history . . . then she'd tell how it affects the rest of literature and society."*) Correlating science and mathematics units would be another example.[48] Perhaps this was done at one time and when things got out of sync, teachers gave up. More likely teachers enjoy teaching material that fascinates them and would resist time constraints being imposed. (I noticed that over the year I observed, the Kennedy assassination and the Vietnam War were subjects that got much more attention in American History class than other events. Probably the middle aged teachers I saw were impacted by both things in their youth. But students did not share this fascination, and complained to me about the duration of the units.) On the face of it, not correlating the timing of the high school curriculum wherever possible seems careless at best, and dismissive of the human need to integrate knowledge at worst. All it would take is time for a conversation among teachers from different departments about when they would like to teach what.[49]

Teachers also need much more time to read in their fields and across diverse fields; they need time to study relevant educational research and teacher narratives. Above all teachers need time to reflect: on themselves as learners, on their relationship to their students and on their students' relationship to the curriculum. (The unavailability of time for reflection and colleague-consulting is what will keep a professor in higher education who might otherwise prefer the spontaneity of adolescents, especially in a state where the salary differential between secondary and higher education is negligible.) Yet this request for more "free" time is declined consistently by administrators and public. One wonders if time spent without an immediately demonstrable product is not a threat to the former and a waste to the latter.

Space use is also affected if large classes are to be cut down to 12 or 15. Schools will have to stay open for longer periods of time, to use the same space twice. We could expect that some students actually would prefer to start school at 7 A.M. if they could finish at noon; others might want to start at noon and finish at 5:00. Students would find their learning enhanced out in the community as apprentices to people who are doing interesting work. Goodlad calls for an "ecosystem of institutions and agencies" that are together responsible for "developing the knowledge, values, skills and habits"[50] of a community. The secondary school is the appropriate locus of that knowledge development. But true community education requires a well-oiled school door that opens both ways. One teacher, a specialist in the emotionally disabled, recommended to me a radical transformation of the school: "[Education] has to move beyond the building . . . into the community and other places. I would just like the building to disappear!" Well the building is not going to disappear; communities that have spent millions updating their school plants are not going to abandon them. But the school could use its space differently on a major scale. The community could use the school sixteen hours a day, not eight. Adults could take classes during the day, while students go into the community to learn. Community members could become part-time teacher-assistants—not in the sense of a parade of visitors with different occupations—but in the sense of sharing a responsibility for the endurance of the culture's traditions, by sharing the teaching under the guidance of master teachers. Perhaps the community could take over some part of the athletic programs which can wreak such havoc on the interpersonal relations in our schools. The suggestion to take athletics out of American high schools surely would be a heresy worthy of a Second Inquisition. But at the very least the community needs a sustained dialogue about the purposes of public education so it can evaluate the contribution of all parts of schooling, even popular ones such as athletics, to those purposes.

In his landmark essay "The Loss of the Creature"[51] Walker Percy muses about what a student takes away from school:

> The educator is well aware that something is wrong, that there is a fatal gap between the student's learning and the student's life. The student reads the poem, appears to understand it and gives all the answers. But what does he recall if he should happen to read a Shakespeare sonnet twenty years later? Does he recall the poem or does he recall the smell of the page and the smell of Miss Hawkins?

What he recalls is a vague feeling of relating to a variety of knowledge in a variety of ways; what he recalls is the feeling of being there. The sonnet, chosen carefully as a treasured artifact of his heritage, is gone, uncommitted to memory, let alone spirit. Inevitably, the question returns to us teachers: How is it students can spend fifteen thousand hours in classrooms and recall so little of what they were intended to know? Are we teaching it wrong, or just asking the wrong questions about it? Or both? Most likely, the questions (superficial) suit the teaching method (transmission of content) which in turn begets the type of questioning (superficial). And the cycle starts all over again. To effect change we should probably start by teaching it differently, but the enthusiasm for that revolution is mute, especially given a stubborn public that will not be weaned off the tasteless, canned formula of standardized tests.

We in education accepted as commonsensical that we would go to society's schools to improve our minds, and then use what we learned for society's good. And yet, after many generations of various (including progressive) runs at improving cognition, do we see an electorate making choices informed by anything more than materialistic considerations? Do we see an increase in creativity? In artistry? In sensitivity? In spirituality? In fraternity? In old-fashioned empathy? Or have we been content to perceive an increase in mental acuity, and tell each other, Problem solved. The postwar years in this country saw a dedication to problem solving that had impressive results, but they were impressive results at an impressive expense.

Statements of educational aim are matters of emphasis at a given time. I believe with Whitehead that the postmodern aim of education is to comprehend that we exist fundamentally in a world that is dynamically interrelated.[52] Teacher and student should sit in a type of campfire circle, a new teaching/learning interaction[53] that will honor various modes of understanding, recognize the individual's insistent present, while striving for the generality of outlook that a community requires for its healthful function. The changes I propose (smaller class size, coordinated course teaching, and community participation in the curriculum and teaching) have little to do with adding subjects, but have a lot to do with altering relationships of people to subjects and to each[54] other. Ultimately the student will *feel* (rather than just cogitate about) the interconnectedness that characterizes life. We have lost that interconnectedness to each other most shockingly in our secondary classrooms, the very place where we counted on our diverse children getting connected. Huge high schools with fragmented curricula, "Tupperware teaching" modes, unforgiving cliques and insistent celebration of athletic prowess over intellectual and artistic power have contributed to that loss, but it is a loss that is reversible. We can begin by taking students' natural interest in communicating with each other and incorporating it as an integral part of the learning environment. The result for them will be a conversation, not always easy or particularly teen-centered. But it will be a conversation that gives students the feeling that they will be required and recognized there; a conversation led by an adult who models a respect for the student world. Many teachers feel they have no time for these whole phenomena, student worlds. But Brian Swimme[55] reminds us that to be human is to live in a story; if so, then we are guilty of neglecting their humanity when we pay students' stories little heed. And we might all despair at the implications of an education that ignores the humanity of its students.

NOTES

1. Whitehead, Alfred North (1929/1967), *The Aims of Education and Other Essays*, NY: Macmillan, p.16.

2. When given a list of regrets about their high school years, 32% of high school students rank, "Should have taken school more seriously" at the top; "Should have enjoyed myself more" is second with 30%. Shell Poll (1999).

3. Geertz, Clifford (1973), *The Interpretation of Cultures*, NY: Basic Books.

4. "But any teacher will tell you that students are not that easily controlled and manipulated. Many students balk at following instruction, and they go out of their way to make life difficult for teachers. Students have an agenda regarding life that might have little to do with the goals of the school," in Spring, Joel (2000), *American Education* (9th ed.), Boston: McGraw Hill.

5. Whitehead, Alfred North,(1938/1966), *Modes of Thought*, Cambridge: Free Press, p.33.

6. Source: Brooks, Mary and Deedra Engmann-Hartung (1976), Austin: Pro-ed..

7. Fleege, O., R. Charlesworth, D.C. Burts, and C.H. Hart (1992): "Stress Begins in Kindergarten: A Look at Behavior During Standardized Testing," in *The Journal of Research in Early Childhood Education, 7* (1), pp.20–25.

8. "Conversation is the way knowledge workers discover what they know, share it with their colleagues, and, in the process create new knowledge for the organization. . . . Conversations-not rank, title, or the trappings of power-determine who is literally and figuratively "in the loop" and who is not," in Webber, Alan, ed. (1993), *Harvard Business Review*, Jan.–Feb., p.28.

9. Creswell, John W. (1998), *Qualitative Inquiry and Research Design: Choosing Among 5 traditions*, Thousand Oaks: Sage, p.19.

10. Oliver, Donald W., with the assistance of Kathleen W. Gershman (1989), *Education, Modernity and Fractured Meaning: Toward a Process Theory of Education*, NY: SUNY Press, p.3.

11. Bateson, Gregory (1972), *Steps to an Ecology of Mind: A Revolutionary Approach to Man's Understanding Himself*, NY: Ballentine, p.xvii.

12. Whitehead, Alfred North (1929/67), *Aims of Education and Other Essays*, NY: Free Press, p.56

13. Although Alfred North Whitehead and Bertrand Russell were close collaborators for a time, they differed about theories of knowing, Russell, an analytic philosopher, telling Whitehead, the speculative philosopher, "I'd rather be narrow-minded than vague and wooly," in Kuntz, Paul Grimley (1984), *Alfred North Whitehead*, Boston: Twayne Publishers, p.50.

14. Whitehead, Alfred North (1938), *Modes of Thought*, NY: Frees Press, p.5.

15. "From the most primitive root, the brainstem, emerged the emotional centers. Millions of years later in evolution, from these emotional centers evolved the thinking brain or "neo-cortex," the great bulb of convoluted tissues that make up the top layers. The fact that the thinking brain grew from the emotional reveals much about the relationship of thought to feeling; there was an emotional brain long before there was a rational one," in Goleman, Daniel (1995), *Emotional Intelligence: Why It Can Matter More than IQ*, NY: Bantam.

16. King, Robert (1988), paper presented at the 10th Annual Bergamo Conference on Curriculum and Theory, Akron, Ohio.

17. To the extent that it has been studied, the relationship of specific engagement behaviors with academic performance is strong and consistent across populations defined by background characteristics and grade level...These studies also have shown that positive engagement behaviors explain why some students perform well in school in spite of the adversities they face as members of high-risk population, that is, they are "academically resilient," in "Class size and Students at Risk: What is Known? What is Next? US Dept of Education Web site: http://www.ed.gov/pubs/ClassSize/practice.html.

18. Rousseau, Jean-Jacques (1956/1973), *The Emile of Jean Jacques Rousseau*, translated by William Boyd, NY: Teachers College Press, p.40.

19. Whitehead, Alfred North (1929/67), *Aims of Education and Other Essays*, NY: Free Press, p.74.

20. Dewey, John (1916/1944), *Democracy and Education* (passim), NY: Capricorn; *Art As Experience* (1934), NY: Martin, Balch and Company, pp.15–16.

21. Greene, Maxine (1978), "Wide-Awakeness and the Moral Life," in *Landscapes of Learning*, NY: Teachers College Press, p.42.

22. Whitehead, Alfred North (1925/1946), *Science and the Modern World*, NY: Free Press, p.199.

23. Percy, William (1957), *Message in the Bottle: How Queer Man Is, How Queer Language Is, And How One Has to Do With the Other*, NY: Farrar, Straus and Giroux, p.57.

24. Mason, Bobbie Ann (1989), *In Country: A Novel*, NY: Harper and Row, p.224.

25. Whitehead, Alfred North (1961), *Adventures of Ideas*, NY: Free Press, p.78.

26. Brumbaugh, Robert (1989),"Whiteheadian American Educational Philosophy," in *Process in Context: Essays in Post-Whiteheadian Perspectives*, Ernest Wolf Gazo, ed., NY: Peter Lang, p.61.

27. Teens spend an average of 4 hours a week on homework and an average of 25 hours a week socializing with their friends. See: Steinberg, Laurence D., with B. Bradford Brown and Sanford M. Dornbusch (1996), *Beyond the Classroom: Why School Reform Has Failed and What Parents Need to Do*, NY: Simon and Schuster, p.178.

28. Falk, Richard (1988), "In Pursuit of the Postmodern," in *Spirituality and Society*, David Ray Griffen (ed.), Albany: SUNY Press, p.87.

29. Bateson, Gregory (1972), *Steps to an Ecology of Mind*, NY: Chandler, p.206. See also Bateson, G., O. Jackson, J. Haley, and J. Weakland (1956) "Toward a Theory of Schizophrenia," *Behavioral Science*, 1, 251–264; and Sue, D., D. Sue and S. Sue (1990): "Double bind theory indicates that contradictory messages sent from parent to child [result] in the child being unable to discern parental meaning. . . . This conflict eventually leads the student to develop difficulty in interpreting other people's communications and in accurately and appropriately conveying his or her own thoughts and feelings," in *Understanding Abnormal Behavior*. Boston: Houghton Mifflin Company, p.407.

30. Percy, William (1957), *The Message in the Bottle: How Queer Man Is, How Queer Language Is, and What One Has to Do With Another*, NY: Farrar, Straus and Giroux, p.5.

31. "Reducing Class Size: What Do We Know?" National Institute on Student Achievement, Curriculum and Assessment, U.S. Department of Education, Report No. SAI-98–3027. Many of the recommendations for school improvement (more experiential, hands-on, active learning, more higher-order thinking, deep study of smaller number of topics and developing the classroom as an interdependent community) would be implemented more easily if classes were down-sized. See: Zemelman, S., H. Daniels and A. Hyde (1998), *Best Practice: New Standards for Teaching and Learning in America's Schools* (2nd Ed.) Portsmouth, NH: Heineman; Daniels, H. and M. Bizar (1996), *Methods that Matter: Six Structures for Best Practice Classrooms*; York: Stenhouse Publishers; and Kohn, A. (1996), "What to Look for in a Classroom," *Educational Leadership*, 54, 1, pp.54–55.

32. "A student's judgment is poorly honed if he merely listens to a dialogue between a teacher and fellow student. Questioning requires a seminar format, a circle of fewer than twenty people. There must be give and take, with the teacher being a participant as well as leader and in no sense a source of "answers . . ." in Sizer, Theodore R. (1985), *Horace's Compromise: The Dilemma of the American High School*, Boston, Houghton Mifflen, p.119.

33. Wilson, James Q. and George L. Kelling (1982), "Broken Windows," *Atlantic Monthly*, 249, 3, pp.29–38.

34. Self-reported sleep times decreased by 40–50 minutes across ages 13–19. The sleep loss was due to increasingly later bedtimes. Students who described themselves

as struggling or failing school (C's, D's/F's) reported that on school nights they obtain about 25 minutes less sleep and go to bed an average of 40 minutes later than A and B students. See Wolfson, Amy R., (1998), "Sleep Schedules and Daytime Functioning in Adolescents, *Child Development, 69,* 4, p.875.

35. A study of undergraduates at Harvard University found that most of the time smaller classes are better, with stronger student engagement. See Light, Richard (2002), *Making the Most of College,* Harvard University Press.

36. "Teachers reported their best experiences in school are those where they connect with students and are able to help them in some way," in Poplin, M. and J. Weeres (1992), *Voices from the Inside: A Report on Schooling from Inside the Classroom,* Claremont, CA: Institute for Education in Transformation, cited in E. Clinchy (ed.) (1999), *Reforming American Education from the Bottom to the Top,* Portsmouth: Heinemann, p.147.

37. McNeal, Ralph (1999), "Participation in High School Extracurricular Activities: Investigating School Effects," *Social Science Quarterly, 80, 2,* p.291.

38. Light, Richard (2002), *Making the Most of College,* Cambridge MA: Harvard University Press.

39. Social interaction plays a fundamental role in the adolescent's development of cognition. Individual student development could not be understood without regard to the social milieu in which the child is imbedded. See Goldstein, Lisa S. (1999), "The Relational Zone: The Role of Caring Relationships in the Co-Construction of Mind," *American Educational Research Journal, 36,* 3, pp.647–673; McDermott, R. P. (1977), "Social Relations as Contexts for Learning in School," *Harvard Educational Review, 47, 2,* 198–213; and Schneider, P. and R.V.Watkins (1996), "Applying Vygotskian Developmental Theory to Language Intervention," *Language, Speech, and Hearing Services in Schools, 27,* pp.157–170.

40. Whitehead, Alfred North (1929/1967), *The Aims of Education and Other Essays,* NY: Free Press, p.55.

41. The problems of the disconnected American high school curriculum can be traced to the university. See Coplin, W.D. (1999) "Higher Education Against the Public Good: How Future Generations Are Conditioned to Serve Only Themselves," in Clinchy, E., ed., *Reforming American Education From the Bottom to the Top.* Portsmouth, NH: Heineman, pp.53–70.

42. Some recent departures in curriculum design bring "emotional literacy" into schools making emotions and social life themselves topics, rather than treating these most compelling facets of a child's day as irrelevant intrusions. See Goleman, G. (1997), *Emotional Intelligence: Why It Can Matter More Than IQ.* NY: Bantam Books, p.263.

43. Students in grades 6–12 in the schools researched here are staffed at 25:1. Exceptions are made depending on the nature of the class.

44. Hunter, Stephan (2000), "As Luck Would Have It: The Real Woody Allen," *International Herald Tribune,* May 22.

45. Brumbaugh, Robert (1982), *Whitehead, Education, and Process Philosophy,* NY: SUNY, p.19.

46. "Time to be thoughtful is what few schools give teachers." Ohanian, Susan (1999), "Is That Penguin Stuffed or Real?" in Clinchy, E., *Reforming American Education from the Bottom to the Top,* Portsmouth, NH: Heinemann, p.26.

47. A field note of mine reads: "We have just come from an English class where they talked about Emerson and Thoreau (19th century) and within five minutes we're in History talking about Coolidge and Henry Ford (20th)."

48. To integrate and streamline the curriculum Sizer recommends 4 subject areas: Inquiry and Expression, Mathematics and Science, Literature and the Arts, Philosophy and History. See: Sizer,Theodore (1984), *Horace's Compromise*, Boston: Houghton Mifflin, p.230. See also "Breaking Ranks: Changing an American Institution," A Report of the National Association of Secondary School Principals on the High School of the 21st Century, Reston, VA, 1996, p.13.

49. Clarke, John H. and Russel M. Agne (1997) *Interdisciplinary High School Teaching: Strategies for Integrated Learning*, Boston: Allyn and Bacon.

50. Goodlad, John (1984), *A Place Called School: Prospects for the Future*, NY: McGraw-Hill, p.361.

51. Percy, Walker (1957), The *Message in the Bottle: How Queer Man Is, How Queer Language Is and What One Has To Do With the Other*, NY: Ferrar, Straus and Giroux, p.57.

52. Whitehead, Alfred North, (1929/1978), *Process and Reality*, corrected edition, David Ray Griffen and Donald W. Sherbourne, eds., NY: Free Press; *Adventures of Ideas* (1933), NY: Free Press; *Modes of Thought* (1938), NY: Free Press.

53. Best Practice's Thirteen Interlocking Principles are that education should be: student-centered, experiential, holistic, authentic, expressive, reflective, social, collaborative, democratic, cognitive, developmental, constructivist and challenging. See: Zemelman, S., Daniels, H, and Hyde, A. (1993), Best *Practice: New Standards for Teaching and Learning in America's Schools* (2nd ed.), Portsmouth: Heineman.

54. "The primary aim of every educational effort must be the maintenance and enhancement of caring," in: Nodding, Nel (1984), *Caring: A Feminine Approach to Ethics & Moral Education*, Berkeley: University of California Press.

55. Swimme, Brian (1988), "The Cosmic Creation Story," in *The Re-enchantment of Science: Postmodern Proposals*, David Ray Griffen, ed., Albany: SUNY Press, p.48.

Chapter Seven

Notes on Methodology

OBSERVATIONS

"Presumably, theory is an enlargement of observation."

Robert Coles[1]

***

"Malinowski had also told us to note down everything we saw and heard since, in the beginning, it is not possible to know what may or may not be significant. I faithfully tried to carry out this injunction, but of course, all observation is selective."

Hortense Powdermaker[2]

I observed classroom behavior and interviewed students in three high schools ("Washington," "Jefferson," and "Madison" High Schools) in two North Dakota cities, continuously over an academic year. A schedule given to me by principals included classes in English, Mathematics, History, Spanish, Distributive Education, Physical Education, Speech, Business Education, Industrial Technology and Art. My goal in the first weeks was to get a rhythm of the school day and learn the ropes of getting around very large buildings on time.

I usually ate lunch in the cafeteria with everybody but conversation with me was not high on students' lists of ways to spend their free 22 minutes, so at the beginning I often sat alone and wrote up the morning's field notes. I remember one day early in the year sitting down at the only empty table in the cafeteria. Since all the other tables were taken I figured students would come along and ask if they could sit at my table and I would eventually have a lunchtime chat with them, a rare treat for me. One by one they came up to the table but they didn't ask to sit with me, they asked if they could borrow a chair! Within ten minutes I was sitting at table of 8 that had only one chair: my own. I should say that after a few months, kids seemed to mind less if we shared a table, especially if I had already interviewed them.

The first few weeks at the site should be marked by close observation and note-taking, as Malinowski suggested to his Anthropology students back in the twenties. But before very long the educational researcher can predict a lot of the class routine. Then the change in the routine, not the routine itself, becomes the object of curiosity: the fact that a teacher would give a pop quiz when the class refuses to discuss the assigned reading, or the fact that everyone in a quiet class starts calling out answers when the question is about something of acute interest to them. Students can be very adept at paying just enough attention to not make a fool of themselves if called on, while at the same time paying another type of attention to other things. So I listened and observed one end of the room, the teacher's end—we'll call it "upstage"—and listened and observed the other end, "downstage," closer to where I was sitting. This is why my notes are full of references to the habits of the back row denizens: I could see them best. The highly motivated students would not always choose to sit back there. There were exceptions to this: we recall the complaint of Sheila (Chapter 2) that the history teacher talked sports with the athletes for the first ten minutes of class, and seemed to have low expectations for the class as a whole. Sheila was a high-achieving student who opted out of participating (*"Anyone who could fail that class, I mean . . ."*) She actually chose to sit at the back, conceding the front to some chatty but low-performing, "teachers' pets."

Classroom observation is like simultaneously watching two stage plays with different plots, and then attempting to write a summary that does justice to them both. My own role as a watcher/listener made me appreciate the dualistic lives of the student in school; but it was our conversations made me understand that one "life," the life of a subculture member, was the story in which they were more invested.

INTERVIEWS

"Thank you for interviewing me."

Christmas card note from Tess, Grade 11

***

"Our lives are passed in the experience of disclosure."

Alfred North Whitehead[3]

I decided I needed four main informants to talk to me every week for background, in addition to a large number of boys and girls who would be willing to talk to me for an hour. The first thing I did was find four girls from different schools who would be sounding boards as I identified patterns of behavior or attitude in the large group. Their individual personalities were striking in their contrast: Tess, the girl with a perfect 4.0 average, a middle child in a large family, who had farm chores, a job, a commitment to her volleyball team, and a future as a teacher of the deaf; Pam, the baby of the family, a dedicated dancer, hardworking, ambitious, but no scholar; Liz, with medications for obsessive-compulsive disorder, a failed track career, a great sense of humor and a step-mother she called her step-monster; and Amber, an only child raised in a female home: mother, grandmother and aunt; sensitive about her Hispanic ethnicity, car*less* (so she walked home from her fast food job at 1 A.M. through a cemetery!) and several grades that bumped along the bottom. I did not know these things about them at first, of course, but after a first interview (where I essentially practiced the protocol I would use later with an additional 96 students) I asked them if they would talk to me individually for an hour every two weeks, and all four agreed. I loved talking to these girls on a regular basis; it was the brightest part of a year that could feel drab. They clarified references to issues and controversies that came up in classes, announcements over the P.A. and in school newspapers; they helped me identify many kids from all different groups to interview (in a population that looked rather more homogeneous than it actually was). And I became friends with them the way researchers always seem to with the main informants of long-term studies.

These four informants might figure a little more prominently in my observations because I couldn't help but notice them if our class schedules overlapped. For instance, the history test where everybody gets into study groups except Tess, (Chapter 3) refers to one of the four girls I interviewed regularly. But even though I talked to them twice a month, the interview material of these four does not actually appear more often than anyone else's because only their first interview was aggregated with the entire database of all interviews with other students.

For the database of 100 interviews, I chose those 50 girls and 50 boys who would represent equally various types of students: "A" students, "average," "artsy," "alienated," and "athletes." "A" students were identified by honor roll lists published in the paper; "average" students came from people making up most of a school's population, a list that I generated myself after several weeks at the various sites. Art students came from art class, orchestra, band or theatre; "alienated" students were those whose appearance would be more unusual; they might be called by their peers, Hippies, Granolas, Grungies, Headbangers or Smokers. Athletes were easy to identify because they had public roles on school teams: hockey, basketball, track, golf and football. Usually I approached people I had been in class with for several weeks; frequently, a student was willing to recommend a friend or acquaintance as an interviewee.

I conducted the interviews, one student at a time, in a room off the library or at a nearby fast food restaurant. I would first give the student a stack of index cards on which were written the names of subjects they had taken or were currently studying. The cards read: English, mathematics, history, biology, chemistry, music, art, theater arts, speech, French, German, Spanish, distributive education, industrial technology and physical education and sports. I asked them to stack up the cards in order of their preference, favorite on top, least favorite on the bottom. Next they were asked to discuss every subject and how they came to put it in its place in the pile. I found that while students could discuss their academic failures and successes easily, their energy in this first part of the interview was singularly absent, as if they were relaying the facts about something that was important to someone they knew well: their brother's track record, for example, or their sister's career plans.

The next part of the interview consisted of ten "prompt" cards[4] which were designed to elicit responses to recent school or personal experiences. The cards read Success, Important to Me, Strong Conviction or Belief, Torn Between, Lost Something, Moved or Touched, Sad, Frustrated, Angry and Anxious. Students took a few minutes to think about these words and to discuss with me just those cards of their choice. It was very rare for someone to choose to say something about all ten words. The most popular card was "Frustrated," the least chosen card was "Success" (and then it was chosen typically to describe a team effort). They claimed to be frustrated by teachers who grade unfairly and by bosses at their after school jobs who treat them unfairly, by drawing up a time schedule that ignored their personal lives. Students who chose "Angry" usually did so because of anger about their classmates' snobbishness, meanness, untrustworthiness or duplicity. Some cards were rarely chosen, e.g., "Strong Conviction" or "Moved/Touched." Many students described the tension between team regulations and the temptations to drink in response to "Torn Between." Everyone chose to answer "Important to me" and it was usually in reference to family and friends, but rarely *school* in the academic sense, only in the group-membership sense. Some cards were misunderstood, e.g., "Anxious" did not always mean "worry" to them. They might respond with, "Yeah, I'm really anxious for the weekend." For "Lost something" they might say, "Uh, I *thought* I lost my script for "Skin of Our Teeth" but I found it under my bed." Before long I changed "Anxious" to "Anxious/Worry" and "Lost Something" to "Lost something/Grief."

After I had done several interviews I realized that the cards were not eliciting a discussion I needed about some topics, such as student cliques or discrimination. I added the following questions:

1. What kids coming to high school for the first time don't realize yet is that . . .
2. What teachers don't know about me is . . .
3. My friends like me because . . .
4. There are groups in my school called by various names such as. . . . They are known for. . . . People might associate me with . . .
5. A new rule in school I would make is . . .
6. True or false: Boys talk more in class because they are smarter.

I adjusted the wording a bit over time as I learned what worked. For example, except for a couple of girls who did say they would make a new rule against cliques, the question about new rules got a poor response. I couldn't understand what was wrong with it until finally one boy said, "Well, no. I could think of some rules I would *eliminate*, maybe, but not any new ones to put in!" So much for the adult's perspective.

Finally, as every researcher has discovered, an interviewee might start sharing more the moment the interviewer turns off the tape-recorder and winds up the session. (This is why you have to allow for write-up time right after an interview before the next appointment, so you can still note the interesting facts from memory.) I remember the day at a fast food restaurant when I was packing away my tape recorder and the boy I was talking to mentioned that there was a small group who called themselves the 900 Club, whose members were intent to consume 900 beers that summer. That figured to be 12 six-packs a week for twelve weeks. We talked a while longer, without the recorder going, about the issue of widespread underage drinking in his town (to which illegality he was indifferent) and later I wrote up that part of the interview from memory. As it turned out, I never got confirmation from any other student about the existence of the club, though I asked about it in remaining interviews. Whether or not this club really existed, he was not going to tell me about it with the tape recorder going.

ANALYSIS

"We do naturalistic research, to speak not of . . . universal forces, but of perceptions and understandings that come from immersion in and holistic regard for the phenomena."

Robert Stake[5]

*** * *

"The abstraction, inherent in the development of language, has its dangers.
It leads away from the realities of the immediate world."

Alfred North Whitehead[6]

My "abstractions," which became the names of the preceding chapters (co-erced, bothered and bewildered) resulted from a three step process: coding, categorizing and finding patterns.[7] A one hour interview yields approximately 20 pages of interview transcript; my data base had over 2,000 pages of typed interview transcripts as well as field notes from observations. Using the soft-ware program "Ethnograph,"[8] I scrolled through the 100 files, each one named for a student whose name had been changed to assure anonymity. I as-signed words or phrases representative of that section of speech to character-ize a unit of data (and any unit can several codes assigned to it). Later, that piece of interviewee's speech could be retrieved and contrasted or compared with others. For example, references to employment or work in all of the 100 interviews, were assigned a code, "job." The program then can copy just those lines about jobs or work or employment from the file, "John Q", and aggregate it with all discussions that were coded with that word across the other 99 interviews. I then read all these excerpts together, looking for a pat-tern. If there are many instances of the code word "frustrated," coexisting with the code "job" it is evidence of a widespread attitude. The co-occurrence of the code "important to me" with the code "friends" was a clear pattern; the incidence of negative comments around curriculum and teaching was its mir-ror opposite. Answers to an open-ended question such as, "What students coming to high school for the first time next fall don't realize yet. . . ." (coded as "sophomore surprise") revealed a broad belief among all students that high school is more challenging ("*started to hurt more*") and changes people ("*thought they knew, they don't know anymore*") when they get there.

Eventually I had a full list of 56 codes that I believe accounted for the most important of their responses; the next step was to collapse that list to a smaller number of categories. A category is an umbrella term for a group of codes; considering the codes' relationships to each other is what gives the category its integrity. Putting codes into categories is necessary not just because you need to work with a smaller number of terms but more importantly because the themes (called "patterned regularities" by Wolcott[9]) in the data will only become apparent to you as you consider how a category contrasts with other categories. This is done by what is called axial coding,[10] i.e., by developing categories in terms of their properties and dimensions. Put another way, the researcher discovers a pattern or key linkage (what Schatzman and Strauss call "the story line")[11] that defines that category.

I first put all codes into one of 2 categories roughly equivalent to "School," meaning curriculum, teaching and learning environment issues; and "Social Lives," meaning social norms, friends and patterns of behavior that were not required, but engaged in. These two categories were not adequate to handle all the personal information students volunteered; students were much more likely to talk about themselves than about school in the abstract sense. So the next working configuration had 3 categories: "Curriculum and Teaching" which had all the codes of school subjects, teachers, tests and homework; "Culture" which had the codes of student groups, norms, parties/drinking, sports, competition and grades; and "Personal" which had the codes of personal goals, self-reports, jobs, family, fun and love. By a constant comparative method, I could see that almost all positive comments were reserved by students for relationships with peers and educators and very few for academic topics like curriculum and teaching. The next set of two categories I named for students' feelings: "Frustrations' and "Freedom," meaning all variations of negative speech and positive speech respectively. I had so much more negative commentary in the Frustration category than positive in the Freedom category, that negative feelings became the bulk of the narrative of this book. The data supporting the Freedom category is in Chapter 5 under sections called "Teacher-as-the Enemy" and "Lessons-as-Important."

The last stage of analyzing data was the most challenging one. (Remember, the schools I researched were famous for quality.) I had anticipated that students would be able to objectify that success, as well as supply me with tips for reforming its few failures. But the students' responses to open questions and prompts were proving to be unenlightening as far as desired betterments were concerned. Reforming school was not something they even thought about. (Hard to believe, since it can obsess people in teacher ed.) When pressed, they just wanted *less of it all:* fewer classes, less homework, no detentions. They wanted the formal part of school to go away (though they would stand six deep in an elective course called "Making Relationships Go Smoother").

Since most of the interviews had fallen into a pattern that described very negative states of mind towards school, except where students mentioned their friends-as-life-saviors, I separated my data into three categories of Perspectives held by Participants. The actual names of the categories were devised by me. The first was Coerced (codes were ideas, teachers pets, teachers' non-pets, rules and minors-in-possession). The key linkage, pattern or "story line" among all codes in that category was the student-feeling-oppressed. The second category was Bothered (codes were bored, angry, stressed, cliques, cheating, drinking and suicide). The key linkage there was the student-feeling-frustrated. The third category was Bewildered (codes were mystified and neglected, including sexism as a form of neglect). The key linkage for this last was the student-feeling-unseen. This is essentially where the analysis ended and the writing began. "All" that was left was to review the data and re-aggregate all of it under these three newly-named categories; write up descriptions of, and my own reflections on, the categories; illustrate them with interview excerpts; and insert classroom vignettes where they supplied good examples of the categories. The last two chapters are Chapter 5, my interpretation of the interview and observational data called, "Two Pathogenic As-Ifs") and Chapter 6, suggestions for remediations called, "Engaging the Disengaged."

NOTES

1. Coles, Robert (1989), *The Call of Stories: Teaching and the Moral Imagination*, Boston: Houghton Mifflin, p.20.

2. Powdermaker, Hortense (1966), *Stranger and Friend: The Way of an Anthropologist*, NY: WW Norton Co., p.61.

3. Whitehead, Alfred North (1938/1966), *Modes of Thought*, NY: Free Press, p.62.

4. I am indebted to Dr. Robert Kegan of the Harvard Graduate School of Education for this interview procedure.

5. Stake, Robert (1978), "The Case Study Method in Social Inquiry," in *Educational Researcher*, Feb., pp.5-8.

6. Whitehead, Alfred North (1938/1966), *Modes of Thought*, NY: Free Press, p.39

7. Bogdan, Robert C. and Sari Knopp Biklan (1982), *Qualitative Research for Education*, Boston: Beacon, p.155; Creswell, John W. (1998), *Qualitative Inquiry and Research Design: Choosing Among Five Traditions*, Thousand Oaks: Sage, pp.56–57; Strauss, Anselm and Juliet Corbin (1998), *Basics of Qualitative Research: Techniques and Procedures for Developing Grounded Theory*, Thousand Oaks: Sage, pp.113–119.

8. Seidel, John (1993), *Ethnograph*, v.3, Thousand Oaks: Scolari.

9. Wolcott, Henry (1994), *Transforming Qualitative Data: Description, Analysis and Interpretation*, Thousand Oaks: Sage.

10. Creswell, John W. (1998), *Qualitative Inquiry and Research Design: Choosing Among Five Traditions*, Thousand Oaks: Sage, p.57; and Strauss, Anselm and Juliet Corbin (1998), *Basics of Qualitative Research: Techniques and Procedures for Developing Grounded Theory*, Thousand Oaks: Sage, p.123.

11. Schatzman, Leonard and Anselm Strauss (1973), *Field Research: Strategies for a Natural Sociology*, Englewood Cliffs, Prentice-Hall, p.111.

Afterword

One reader of the preceding pages might say that the student complaints are real and true, 22% of students do feel disengaged in school, but so what? Someone should tell these kids to pull up their socks and get going. Basically this response says, no one ever promised them a rose garden when they went off to first grade. School Is Work, and it will ever be thus. Another reader might say that the interviews exaggerate the real situation, that given the opportunity kids will complain about school to any adult who listens to them non-judgmentally. Basically this response says, we can't really take all the complaints seriously, kids always will prefer each other's company to studying. Students Are Whiners, and they will ever be thus.

I think that both responses let adults off the hook for examining a situation that, at best, could make more of a big expensive effort and at worst, could be dangerous for participants in it. I don't think the School-Is-Work response does justice to the genuine problems with pedagogy that I observed. Telling kids to toughen up does nothing to call to account the indifferent or burnt-out teacher. Although I am a good old fashioned progressive (speaking oxymoronically), I see no contradiction between that philosophy and maintaining high expectations for every student; I believe kids value their accomplishments more if they work hard at them. But teachers themselves have to work too, particularly at engaging the learner. It's true that students should meet them half way; and it's true that administrators could arrange for more time for reflection, for democratic action, for curriculum coordination, and peer reviews of practice. But when all is said and done, as Eva Brann put it, "The effort of a single teacher is the ultimate resort of excellence in education."[1]

Nor am I sure the Students-Are-Whiners response does justice to the sincerity I felt as I listened to these students. Not every student felt every emotion, every day that they describe in the preceding pages but all would recognize the emotions as ones experienced by the members of their group. What their group has in common is feeling as though the curriculum is something they generally *come up against*, as opposed to something they construct with relish. The exceptions to this negativity are those classes where they pick up enough wind in their sails to lift them over choppy waters of the rest of the day. Everyone had classes he looked forward to, due to the happy coincidence of his natural proclivity and excellent pedagogy. But—and this is the important consideration— given the chance to describe the curriculum and instruction of their schooling for an hour, students referred to excellent classes very little. When this type of "success" is glossed-over again and again, and when these students are interviewed apart from each other, we have to consider that their negative feelings are genuine, even if sporadic. These feelings interfere, to put it mildly, with true apprehension of the curriculum.

Generating interpretations of others' perspective is inherently a matter of inference from descriptions of behavior, whether the data are derived from observations, interviews, or some other source.[2] Generalizing beyond the three sites I visited to high schools everywhere would be problematic, but I do hope and believe the findings will be of interest to those who deal with teenagers in a school setting, no matter the size or diversity of the population there.

NOTES

1. Brann, Eva T.H. (1979), *Paradoxes of Education in a Republic*, Chicago: University of Chicago Press, p.5.

2. Maxwell, Joseph A. (1996), *Qualitative Research Design: An Interactive Approach*, Thousand Oaks: Sage.

Index